R00232 46528

HAR

D0936630

KF   Parker, Frank
224   J. 1940—
.C44
P37   Caryl Chessman, the
cop. 4   red light bandit

DATE			

THE CHICAGO PUBLIC LIBRARY

SOCIAL SCIENCES AND HISTORY DIVISION

© THE BAKER & TAYLOR CO.

CARYL CHESSMAN:
The
Red Light
Bandit

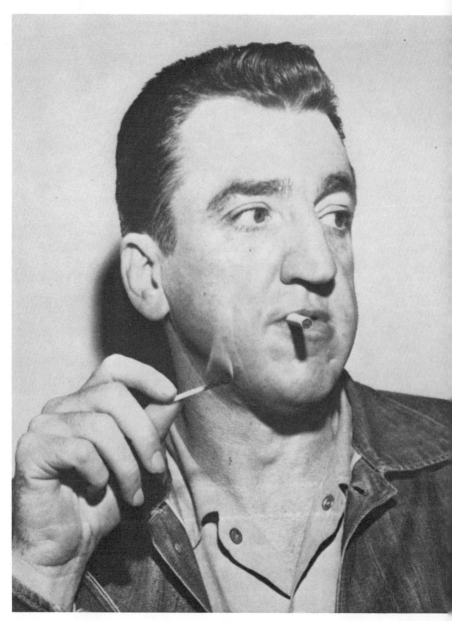

UPI Telephe

CARYL CHESSMAN:

The

Red Light

Bandit

Frank J. Parker

Nelson-Hall • **Chicago**

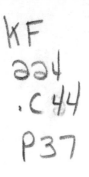

KF
224
.C44
P37

cop. 4
Soc

Library of Congress Cataloging in Publication Data

Parker, Frank J   1940-
  Caryl Chessman: The red light bandit

  Bibliography: p.
  Includes index.
  1. Chessman, Caryl, 1921-1960.   I. Title.
KF224.C44P37   345'.73'02523   75-8760
ISBN 0-88229-188-2

Copyright © 1975 by Frank J. Parker

All rights reserved. No part of this book may be reproduced
in any form without permission in writing from the publisher,
except by a reviewer who wishes to quote brief passages in
connection with a review written for broadcast or for inclusion
in a magazine or newspaper. For information address Nelson-Hall
Inc., Publishers, 325 W. Jackson Blvd., Chicago, Illinois 60606.

Manufactured in the United States of America.

To my parents

And he that stealeth a man,
and selleth him,
or if he be found in his hand,
he shall surely be put to death.

—Exodus 21:16

Contents

Acknowledgments

Recently, I stumbled across a book in which the author objected to the increasing, depressing tendency to acknowledge the assistance in book preparation of everyone who chipped in a paper clip. Perhaps he is right; yet without a paper clip pages fly away. Without the desired small piece of information, the work is that much less complete. So, I will plead guilty of wanting to recognize everyone who assisted in matters small and large. United States Supreme Court Justice Tom C. Clark; Los Angeles Municipal Court Judge Gilbert C. Alston; Richard Levine, former librarian of the United States Court of Appeals in New York; Thomas Cole, official reporter of the New York Supreme Court in Manhattan; California Deputy Attorney General Arlo C. Smith and his secretary, Vida Allen; Vida Ryan, California Department of Corrections Statistician; Abe L. Wirin, Esq.; Editorial Veechi of Rio de Janeiro; Professor Charles E. Rice, Notre Dame Law School; Professor David Twomey, Boston College; Ted Carey, M.D.; and the librarians of the Belgian Ministry of Foreign Affairs.

I would be greatly remiss if I did not give special thanks to all of the following. In very real measure, the present study could not

have been completed without their detailed, thorough cooperation. The officers of the National District Attorneys Association,
President Carol Vance, Executive Director Patrick Healy, and
Project Director James Heelan, provided me with a letter of
introduction to Los Angeles County District Attorney Joseph
Busch. Their interest and encouragement was matched by that of
Mr. Busch and his staff. There is a lot of talk about press
censorship these days. None of it applies to either of these fine
organizations.

By a quirk of fate, J. Miller Leavy, the man who prosecuted
Caryl Chessman in 1948 and was his great adversary during the
dozen remaining years of Chessman's life, today is Director of
Operations in the Los Angeles County District Attorney's Office.
I did Mr. Leavy a great injustice by assuming beforehand that his
cooperation would be at best lukewarm. As it turned out, I could
not have been better treated if my purpose was to be his
biographer. I spent a most pleasant month in his office. All my
questions were answered; all desired records provided; much
background information supplied; and a lot of sophisticated
discussion of criminal law provided free of charge. Leavy has a
central role in this case. As my book will show, I do not always
agree with Leavy's actions in the Chessman case. At the same
time, I respect him and his desire to do justice as he sees it. Leavy
often said to me, "You will be like all the rest; tell me I am a
great guy to my face and then knife me in your book." Perhaps
he will think so. I care enough for his respect to hope not.

Full cooperation also was rendered to me by Chessman's two
principal attorneys, George T. Davis and Rosalie Asher, and by
the Chairman of the State Board of Equalization, William
Bennett and San Quentin Warden Louis Nelson. All were deeply
involved in the Chessman case. Each tried to be of maximum
assistance. All made available to me records otherwise unavail-
able.

Since I wrote most of this book while living in Belgium, I am
particularly grateful to two librarians at the Belgium National
Library, American Studies Center in Brussels; Madame La
Gangée and Madame Grötjans. These ladies and their relentless
Telex machine arranged to have sent to me by interlibrary loan

books on the subject from such diverse spots as Vienna, Madrid, Paris, and Copenhagen. Even more important, their interest and encouragement carried me over many moments of discouragement. In like manner, the nine Cuban and Belgian Jesuits with whom I lived in Louvain often did my share of the cooking and dishes so I could eat, live, and sleep the story of Caryl Whittier Chessman.

Finally, my father, Frank J. Parker, interrupted his pleasant retirement days of swimming and reading the financial news to revert to his glory days as United States Attorney in Brooklyn and did much of the backbreaking legal research that I was unable to do because of my overseas location. He is in large measure responsible for whatever merit this work has. I also wish to thank my typist Barbara Casavant, and Bill Hickey, who taught me more law in the year we taught together at Boston College than I learned from all my law school professors together.

Naturally, the familiar statement about all errors and opinions being mine alone applies to this work.

A *Propos* of Hanging*

Whilst the Shah of Persia was on a visit to England, he wanted to see how the English executed their criminals. The sight of torture is a favorite entertainment of Eastern monarchs. Accompanied by a numerous suite, he went to Newgate, the London *Roquette*. Great was his disappointment upon hearing that the rope gave instantaneous death. However, he decided upon seeing how the apparatus worked, and desired the governor of the prison to be good enough to execute a criminal on the spot. It was represented to him that there were no criminals lying under sentence of death just then. He was about to lose his temper, when, recollecting himself, he cried, "That's no objection; I will let you have one of my suite."

The London folks have not forgotten it yet.

*Max O'Rell, *John Bull and His Island* (London: The Leadenhall Press, 1882), pp. 110-11.

part 1

The Legal Lynching of Caryl Chessman

The End of the Chessman Case

The cyanide pellets were dropped into the pan of acid at 10:30 A.M. The "red light bandit," Caryl Chessman, was dead within nine minutes. His last moments of life were in character with the role he played during his twelve-year battle to escape the San Quentin gas chamber.

A guard instructed Chessman to breathe quickly and deeply once the poisonous gas started to envelop the little green room. Chessman had never obeyed law enforcement officers before in his life, and he did not do so at the end. Spurning all advice, he held his breath for over a minute. As a result, his death was likely more painful than necessary. The very act of grasping for life by holding his last breath of clean air is significantly typical of Chessman. He had fought stubbornly at each step toward the gas chamber, seizing every opportunity the law provided. Few individuals had succeeded as well as Chessman in forcing the corporate state to devote its attention to one citizen.

The legal machinery that cranked so fitfully for twelve years was still turning at the end. Chessman once said that he had no more lives than a cat; he would not survive his ninth appointment with death. He was within thirty seconds of being wrong. As his execution started, the secretary to United States District Judge, Louis E. Goodman, was in the process of telephoning San Quentin to relay the order of the judge that the execution be postponed until he had time to read and reflect upon the latest set of arguments advanced by Chessman's lawyers. This would have been the ninth official postponement of execution.

In reality, had Goodman halted the execution, the stay would have been only temporary. His action was reviewable by the United States Supreme Court Justice responsible for that district, William O. Douglas. Presented with the petition at the same time that Goodman was, Douglas instantly rejected it. Those surprised by this action of the traditional superliberal forget his Midwestern background, his general rigidness on sex crime cases, and his irritation with Chessman's legal manipulations. In 1957, Douglas had charged that Chessman was "playing a game with the courts."

The American legal system could not even complete the execution of Chessman without uncertainty and mistake. The secretary misdialed San Quentin on the first attempt. Whether the few seconds which this mistake claimed would have made a difference is questionable. Yet this lack of precision has a definite place in the history of the Chessman case as it characterizes all the other governmental mistakes and acts of inefficiency.

A quarter of a century has passed since the trial of Caryl Chessman. This is the second decade since his execution. Why dig up the case? California no longer has a death penalty. Unless the law changes again, no one else will mount the carpeted stairs to meet a premature end. Is there justification for a book on this subject now? Obviously, because I have spent much time and effort in writing one on this California death penalty case, I am not going to say no. However, to be valid, my reasons must be more substantial than mere personal pride.

There have been numerous books on the case. Most obvious are Chessman's own books, all written in prison and smuggled out: an autobiography, *Cell 2455, Death Row*, published in 1954, and two books based on his legal battles, *Trial by Ordeal* (1955) and *The Face of Justice* (1957). These books were widely read and

Cell 2455, Death Row was translated into eighteen languages and sold roughly half a million copies throughout the world. In addition, shortly after Chessman's death, a writer and an editor of *Argosy* magazine, Milton Machlin and William Read Woodfield, published an argumentative book on the case, *Ninth Life* (1961). This book pillories the whole California system of justice and argues that Chessman was convicted for crimes committed by another man, Charles Terranova. Also published in 1961 (and recently reprinted) is an analysis of the trial by lawyer William M. Kunstler, *Beyond a Reasonable Doubt? The Original Trial of Caryl Chessman.* In the period just prior to the execution there were a flurry of books and articles about the Chessman case. One of these, *Chessman M'a Dit* (1960) by Dominique La Pierre, is mentioned several times in this book. La Pierre is an able and successful writer on current topics, and in my opinion the Chessman book is the only bad one he ever wrote. But it *is* a bad book. It is clear that he knew virtually nothing about the American legal system, and absolutely nothing about the Chessman case. To a lesser degree one has the same sense about most of the books written in the heat of pre-execution agitation, books such as Julio Camerero's *Yo Hable Con Chessman* (1960).

Caryl Whittier Chessman was accused of being the "red light bandit." He was charged with committing robbery, kidnapping, attempted rape, and unnatural sexual acts in January 1948 in the Los Angeles area. There were eighteen charges, and at the trial in the spring of 1948, Chessman was convicted on seventeen counts, two of them carrying the death penalty. But the "red light bandit" never murdered anyone; never raped anyone in the conventional sense of the word; never mutilated anyone; and it is highly questionable if he ever sent anyone to an insane asylum. Yet the belief that Chessman did some or all of these things was responsible for his eventual execution. In fact, the four myths live on today.

It is a long step in California from a sentence of death to actual execution. In the fifteen-year period from 1942 through 1956, 180 people were condemned to death in California. Less than two-thirds actually were executed. All but one of those executed during this period had taken the life of someone else. This very statistic strongly suggests that Chessman would not have been executed if factual misstatements had not created such a strong public outcry for his execution. This public mood clearly, but improperly, affected Chessman's fate.

The facts in the case were available for all to see; too many people ignored them, inexcusably. Any hope for an objective portrayal in this book depends on a clear comprehension of the facts. So that the reader can have easy access to the events, dates, and names, a chronology appears at the end of this book. But then we must go beyond the chronology to evaluate the events described. Our starting point will be the eighteen felony counts for which Chessman stood trial. After a consideration of them, we will examine the actions of the key figures in the case and assess the propriety and justice of those acts. It will soon be clear that I have little liking for Chessman, but believe he should not have been executed, that I find many mistakes in the legal process that brought him to death, but find few who were conscious villains.

American justice prides itself on being the best in the world. The true test of this will always be the way it handles difficult cases. Indisputably, the Chessman case must be rated among the most difficult cases in American legal history. By analyzing various elements in the case to see whether things were handled justly and properly, we can perhaps locate both the successes and failures of this case and apply our understanding to the problems of today. Only by facing both the good and the bad in our past actions can we hope to improve our system of justice. Caryl Chessman is long dead; all the words in the world will not bring him back to life. Many of those who toiled so assiduously to bring the life of Chessman to a premature end have, likewise, passed from the earth. Only our form of government, our legal system, remains. For this reason, it is hoped that Caryl Chessman can still be the source of some good for society.

2

The "Red Light" Crimes

In a ninety-four-hour period between 4:30 A.M. Sunday, January 18, 1948, and 2 A.M. four days later, there were five separate criminal incidents involving a man driving a late model Ford with a flashing red light. These were the so-called "red light" crimes. Caryl Chessman was arrested on January 23, and the State of California charged that he was the "red light bandit."

Thomas Bartle, a young dentist, and Miss Ann Plaskowitz were driving along the Pacific Coast Highway near Malibu at 4:30 A.M. on January 18, a Sunday. A late model Ford started to follow them. After a few moments of pursuit, someone in the Ford began to flash a red light which was reflected in the rear view mirror of Bartle's car. Thinking it was the police, he pulled to a stop. Instead of a badge, the man produced a gun and demanded money. Bartle gave him $15 from his wallet. The assailant was not masked. The dentist described the robber to the police as being stocky, five-feet six-inches tall, weighing 150 pounds, and possessing crooked front teeth. When Chessman was later shown to the dentist for identification purposes, he unhesitatingly fingered the suspect. The fact that Chessman wore a bridge and, thus, had extremely straight front teeth—and that

Chessman was six feet tall and a well-proportioned 170 pounds—did not deter the dentist in the slightest.

Thirteen hours after the first incident, the red light flashed again. Floyd Ballew, an automobile salesman from Custer, Oklahoma, and Miss Elaine Bushaw were parked on a lonely road overlooking the Rose Bowl in Pasadena. This couple also assumed that the man emerging from the Ford was a policeman. He carried a .45 automatic and a pen-type flashlight. Even though it was only 5:30 P.M., it was January and, consequently, quite dark. The bandit took $20 from Ballew. He neglected Miss Bushaw's purse that was resting in plain view on the back seat. The bandit was not masked. He saw Miss Bushaw trying to memorize his facial features and he gave her a hard slap. Later the couple described their assailant to police as being five-feet seven-inches tall and weighing 150 pounds. Later, at a line up, they both identified Chessman, at least in a general manner.

Twenty-six hours later on Monday, January 19, 1948, at 7:30 P.M., the "red light bandit" struck again. This time the victims were a thirty-four-year-old Navy veteran, Jarnigan Lea, and a neighbor, Mrs. Regina Johnson, a pretty mother of a thirteen-year-old girl. The Johnson family did not own a car. When Lea, an old Navy friend of Mr. Johnson, invited the Johnsons to take a ride, Mr. Johnson declined the invitation, preferring to watch television, but told his wife to keep Lea company. They were parked on a hill possessing a fine view of Los Angeles in the distance.

The only difference between this and the other two incidents was that the assailant was masked. The Ford, red spotlight, gun, and pen-type flashlight all were present. Lea handed over his wallet containing somewhere between $35 and $50. Mrs. Johnson held out her purse to the bandit; he spurned it. Instead he ordered her to accompany him to his car. Lea protested that Mrs. Johnson suffered from polio and had been released from the hospital only a few days before. Actually this was not totally accurate. It was three years since Mrs. Johnson had been stricken with polio. Still, in the pre-Salk vaccine days suffering could be intense; and Mrs. Johnson's later claims that she had great difficulty in navigating the twenty-two feet to the car of the assailant cannot automatically be discounted. At the trial, the prosecutor emphasized the suffering of this forced march and the poor health of the woman must have won sympathy for her in the eyes of the jury.

At gunpoint, Mrs. Johnson was ordered to remove her underclothes; however, she was menstruating. The bandit exposed himself and ordered her to perform an action known euphemistically as "oral intercourse," medically as "fellatio," and in Section 288a of the penal code of the state of California as "an unnatural sexual act." Fearing for her life, she did as ordered. As the act was being completed, a car of teenagers drove by. The quick-thinking Mrs. Johnson told the still-masked assailant that it might be the police. Fearing to be seen by them while masked, he pulled the mask off. This allowed Mrs. Johnson to view his face at point-blank range.

The bandit took $5 from her purse and sent her back to Lea. Originally, he had taken Lea's car keys, and he had threatened to harm Mrs. Johnson if Lea moved from the front seat of his car. Thus, the fact that Lea had remained in his own car during the incident was justifiable and prudent. Upon returning to the car, Mrs. Johnson was hysterical. Her hysteria is quite understandable. But this brings into question the reliability of both the identification and the details of the story as she later related them.

As to the identification, certainly she had the opportunity for a clear view of the attacker's face. The jury, by recommending the death penalty, demonstrated belief in the reliability of this identification. The unshakable conviction of the mature, attractive, violated woman that the defendant was the perpetrator must have completely negated all of Chessman's efforts to prove his innocence. But there is more to the problem than this. In her first account to the police, Mrs. Johnson only said that she was ordered to perform oral intercourse, and that just at that time the car of teenagers arrived. Soon after the execution of Chessman, Machlin and Woodfield's *Ninth Life* challenged Mrs. Johnson's trial testimony that the "red light bandit" forced her to perform the act. They deduced from her first account that the teenagers arrived *before* it could be carried out. This is a most serious accusation, for without at least a forced attempt at oral intercourse, one of the elements—bodily harm—required for the crime carrying the death penalty would be missing. Furthermore, Machlin and Woodfield charged that the prosecution hid the first Johnson report and never made the defendant aware of its existence.

In both cases, Machlin and Woodfield, who are obviously pro-Chessman, seem to be stretching the facts to fit their view. Little should be made of the fact that Mrs. Johnson did not supply precise details in her first account. It seems more than likely that she was still suffering from emotional shock at the time of her first interview with the police, which took place only a few hours after the attack. She was in no condition to give exact details at that time. Also, one would assume that the police did not press her to give particulars on the attack at that point. Their main interest would have been to obtain an accurate description so they could apprehend the assailant. The charge that the prosecution withheld the first police report will be discussed later, but here it should be said that it seems only natural that the more complete and precise police report would be the one introduced into evidence.

Jarnigan Lea backed Mrs. Johnson's story both as to identification and to the fact that oral intercourse had taken place. Lea unhesitatingly identified Chessman even though he readily admitted to never having seen him unmasked. In addition, Lea had originally described the assailant as being between five-feet eight-inches and five-feet nine-inches tall, three to four inches shorter than the six-foot-tall Chessman. As to the oral intercourse, Lea maintained that he saw semen on the coat of Mrs. Johnson when she returned to his car. Chessman never could shake Lea in his belief that it was seminal fluid. But law enforcement officials neglected to have chemical tests made on the coat, so no substantive proof existed that there was seminal fluid on her coat.

Chessman made much of the police failure to test the coat for semen during his argument to the jury. The prosecutor tried to play down the importance of having chemical tests done, saying the prosecution could not think of everything. It was claimed that such tests could not link the semen to any one man. Medically, it is indeed possible to tell if the specimen in question belongs to the defendant. There was no valid excuse for not making the test, even if a great deal of other evidence existed. Still this carelessness gave pro-Chessman forces an argument that they, otherwise, would not have had.

That same evening, January 19, the red light flashed again. This time it was in the lonely Laurel Canyon area. The unlucky parked couple were Gerald Stone, a truck salesman, and Esther Panasuk, a Pan-American stewardess from Manila. This fourth incident was relatively minor in nature. The bandit settled for the dollar in change belonging to Stone and the single dollar bill belonging to the stewardess. The handkerchief mask slipped from the face of the bandit during this holdup. Of the two, only Stone was asked to identify Chessman (Miss Panasuk had returned to the Philippines), and he refused to identify either Chessman or the automobile. This victim had originally described the robber as being six feet tall and weighing 180 pounds. For once, the description tallied with that of Chessman. Yet Stone would say no more than that Chessman looked something like the bandit. Stone was sure that it was not the same car as the one that the police linked to Chessman. Stone never testified at the trial of Chessman. The conviction on this count was predicated totally on a disputed confession by Chessman, and the fact that the robber wore a handkerchief mask, carried a gun and a pen-type flashlight, and used a Ford with a flashing red light.

Two nights after the Johnson and Stone cases, seventeen-year-old Mary Alice Meza and her college-student companion, Frank Hurlburt, were parked on a lonely road near Los Angeles. The time was 1:30 A.M. on January 22. A masked bandit emerged from a Ford carrying a gun and a pen-type flashlight. The thoroughly terrified couple had no money. Mary Alice was ordered to get into the Ford. This time the assailant chose to drive away. She was in his custody over two hours. During this time he stopped the car and forced her to undress. Rape was attempted; however, like Mrs. Johnson, Mary Alice also was menstruating. In addition, she was a virgin. The assailant gave up the attempt and instead forced her to perform oral intercourse. Finally he drove the thoroughly hysterical girl back to the vicinity of her house.

Three days after the Meza attack, Chessman was brought to the house of the convalescing girl for identification purposes. A rash and swelling that apparently was the result of a nervous reaction had blown her face up to double its normal size so that her eyes were virtually swollen shut. The doctor had ordered her to stay in her room. Chessman was left standing on the sidewalk in the custody of one policeman. The prisoner probably did not look much better at this point than Mary Alice. He had been in custody overnight. To hear him tell it, he had been beaten brutally. In any event, he had not been allowed to shave, wash, or change his clothes. He must have presented quite a contrast to his neatly dressed custodian.

At the urging of the other policeman, Mary Alice looked out her window at the suspect. The house was about fifty feet from the sidewalk where Chessman stood. From her second-floor observation point, she identified Chessman as her attacker. At the trial, she repeated her identification and added the fact that after her attack, the assailant had telephoned her and threatened physical harm if she told anyone that she had been attacked. She insisted that the voice on the phone sounded exactly like that of Chessman.

Can the identification of Mary Alice be trusted? The answer is probably not. This does not mean that the attacker was not Chessman—only that it is doubtful whether she could tell or not. Originally she and her companion, Frank Hurlburt, had both placed the height of the attacker at five-feet seven-inches. Rather improbably, she maintained that the attacker never lowered his mask. This would mean he drove around the streets of Los Angeles for over two hours while wearing a mask. It also means that it would be much harder for her to identify accurately the face of the attacker. This is in addition to the circumstances existing on the day of identification. Her inflamed face, swollen eyes, shaken nerves, and distance from the prominently displayed Chessman, all raise a grave question as to the accuracy of her second-floor window identification. Significantly, Hurlburt never would support her allegation by identifying Chessman. Thus her story had little corroboration. No doubt, a particularly ghastly crime occurred; however, it seems to have been beyond the competence of Mary Alice to say it was perpetrated by Chessman.

In *Ninth Life*, Machlin and Woodfield went farther in questioning Mary Alice's testimony. They noted discrepancies, as in the Johnson case, between the first statement to the police and the one entered as evidence in the trial. They made much over some slight confusion by Mary Alice as to whether the attack took place in the back or front seat. They also drew attention to the fact that she stated that she did not know if intercourse had been completed or not. Granted, these details add to the picture of her confusion and cast further doubt on her ability to identify Chessman accurately. However, they certainly do not indicate that an attack never occurred, as the authors try to hint. The hysteria of the young girl could totally cloud specific details. As to her uncertainty if intercourse in a medical sense had occurred, it must be remembered that she was a virgin. Medical examination several hours after Mary Alice arrived home on the morning of January 22 clearly indicated bruising in the region of the vagina, but that the hymen was still intact. Chessman tried to show in cross examination that the bruises might have been caused by a finger. But it seems fairly clear that while intercourse had not been complete, it certainly had been attempted.

Eighteen months after the attack, the doors of Camarillo State Hospital, a mental institution, closed behind Mary Alice, probably forever. The diagnosis was incurable schizophrenia. She had totally withdrawn from reality and was convinced that everyone was persecuting her. Psychiatric testimony indicates that the mental illness existed *before* the attack, and that her complete breakdown would have occurred regardless of the attack and the accompanying courtroom appearance of a nerve-wracking nature. True as this may be, absolutely no one would believe it. Until his dying day, virtually every opponent of Chessman asserted that the vicious attack on this girl drove her into permanent insanity.

Mary Alice Meza is the tragic figure in the whole affair. She was so youthful, gentle, beautiful in a way resembling a young Paulette Goddard. There are no more pathetic words in the whole case than those to her attacker: "Why are you doing this to me? I never did anything to you." A recounting of the Chessman case often resembles the script of a particularly bad Hollywood grade

"B" film of the fifties. The hysteria and melodrama should not blot out the fact that real people were involved and that real suffering occurred.

But some of the emotion connected with Mary Alice was contrived or exaggerated and it tended to poison the air against Chessman. For instance, although Mary Alice had been with Hurlburt at least one previous time, and perhaps with other boys, newspapermen could not help putting into their stories the heart-rending detail that January 22 had been her first date. And in later years Mary Alice's mother vented her grief by saying that only by the execution of Chessman would her daughter be cured. Like prairie wildfire, the rumor spread that Mary Alice's psychiatrist believed that the execution of Chessman would cure the girl. And there was no way that Chessman could combat these false stories. Surely they fanned the flames of public hatred of Chessman, but just as surely none of the outcry helped Mary Alice.

The police were slow to find the link that connected the five incidents. It was not until the red light had flashed five times in a four-day period that the connection was made. At this point, about 6 P.M. Friday, January 23, a general description of the bandit and his Ford was carried as a bulletin on the police teletype.

Shortly after that bulletin went out there was a holdup of a men's clothing store in Redondo Beach, a small resort town twenty miles south of Hollywood. Two men walked into Town Clothiers at 6:30 P.M. and, after a short interval, pulled out pistols and forced the proprietor, Melvin Waisler, and his clerk, Joe Lescher, to walk into the storeroom in the back. The shorter of the holdup men gave Waisler a vicious chop on the forehead with his pistol, producing a wound which took six stitches to close. The robbers helped themselves to $300 in clothes, Lescher's wallet that contained $38, and $227.30 from the cash register.

About 8 P.M. that same Friday evening, two Los Angeles policemen spotted a car and driver that seemed to fit the teletype description driving down Vermont Avenue. The officers, John Riordan and Robert May, gave chase in their squad car. What happened from there on in is and was highly disputed. The policemen claimed that the driver of the Ford went into a gas station and drove through the pump area without stopping. Instead he picked up speed. At times his speed reached ninety miles per hour. The policemen radioed for assistance and fired at the fleeing car. Finally, the Ford was wedged in and forced to come to a crashing halt. A second man in the wrecked Ford jumped out, but surrendered immediately. He was David H. Knowles. The driver threw a pistol on the street and at the same time took off on the run, in the opposite direction. Officer May, gun in hand, followed in hot pursuit. Two shots were fired by May. One may have nicked the fleeing fugitive. In any event, he fell to the ground and was swiftly apprehended. This was Caryl Chessman.

The haul in the car was quite illuminating: A .45 caliber pistol, a pen-type flashlight in working order, a toy pistol, clothing worth $300 taken from a clothing store in Redondo Beach, and the wallet of the clerk in the store were all discovered by the police while searching the Ford. The Ford proved to be stolen. Three false license plates also were found. In Chessman's pocket were found a nut and wire that police later theorized might have been used to attach a piece of red cellophane to the outside white spotlight of the Ford. Chessman always maintained the nut and wire were planted by police.

At a police lineup, Waisler and Lescher identified the six-foot Chessman and the five-foot eight-inch Knowles as the two robbers. The robbers had not worn masks at Redondo Beach. Both victims were positive that it was the mustached Knowles who had forced them into the back room and struck Waisler. Chessman and Knowles had been apprehended at 8 P.M.; this would have given them enough time to return to Los Angeles from Redondo Beach after the 6:30 P.M. robbery.

After the arrest of Chessman, three other criminal violations were attributed to him. Mrs. Rose K. Howell of South Pasadena claimed that the Ford in question was her car, stolen on January 13. Mrs. Mary Tarro, a neighbor of Chessman's mother, identified Chessman as the man she had surprised in the act of either climbing in or out of her ground-floor window at 8 P.M. on January 17. Finally, Donald McCullough, a young clerk in the

Pasadena clothing store of Carl Hoeschler, identified Chessman and Knowles as the unmasked armed robbers of that store at 7 P.M. on January 3. The only discrepancy in his account was that he insisted the taller man, Chessman, wore the mustache. This discrepancy was never picked up by Chessman at his trial. The amount of money taken from the Pasadena clothing store was $500 in cash and $300 in checks. McCullough was not beaten or forced to move during the robbery.

About four weeks after Chessman's arrest he was arraigned. There were eighteen charges against him, shown in the list below. Most of the charges are self-explanatory (first degree robbery, attempted robbery, and so on). The Sec. 288 unnatural act charge refers to the alleged oral intercourse. The one charge that needs explanation is the kidnapping Sec. 209 charge. Later in this book Sec. 209 will be discussed at length. But the reader should know now that it is a part of the kidnapping law where at least robbery and possibly bodily harm, but no ransom demand, are present. In 1948 Sec. 209 could carry the death penalty under certain circumstances.

Today, with the advantage of hindsight, it is clear that four large areas of controversy existed in the Chessman affair. Much of the terrible confusion and acrimony that occurred could have been avoided if those involved in the case had been able to distinguish the various contested areas and deal with each separately. This did not happen. The issues were so hopelessly tangled and intertwined that the lack of clarity that occurred was inevitable. It is absolutely impossible to reach correct answers if the governing questions are badly posed. Sifting through the debris twenty-five years later, it is my intention to try illuminating the Chessman case by a careful posing of the questions pertaining to the following problems:

1. Was Caryl Chessman the "red light bandit"?
2. Was he proven guilty beyond a reasonable doubt at a fair trial?
3. Should Caryl Chessman have been executed?
4. Did an adequate trial transcript exist so as to provide Chessman with a fair appellate review of his conviction, as required by law?

The Charges against Caryl Chessman

	Date of Offense	Victim	Charge	Verdict	Sentence
1.	1-3-48	D. McCullough	Robbery 1	Guilty	
2.	1-13-48	R. Howell	Auto Grand Theft	Guilty	
3.	1-17-48	M. Tarro	Breaking and Entering	Innocent	
4.	1-18-48	T. Bartle	Robbery 1	Guilty	
5.	1-18-48	F. Ballew	Robbery 1	Guilty	
6.	1-19-48	J. Lea	Robbery 1	Guilty	
7.	1-19-48	R. Johnson	Robbery 1	Guilty	
8.	1-19-48	R. Johnson	Sec. 209 Kidnapping	Guilty	Death
9.	1-19-48	R. Johnson	Sec. 288 Unnatural Act	Guilty	
10.	1-20-48	G. Stone	Robbery 1	Guilty	
11.	1-22-48	F. Hurlburt	Attempted Robbery	Guilty	
12.	1-22-48	M. Meza	Sec. 209 Kidnapping	Guilty	Death
13.	1-22-48	M. Meza	Attempted Rape	Guilty	
14.	1-22-48	M. Meza	Sec. 288 Unnatural Act	Guilty	
15.	1-23-48	M. Waisler	Robbery 1	Guilty	
16.	1-23-48	J. Lescher	Robbery 1	Guilty	
17.	1-23-48	M. Waisler	Sec. 209 Kidnapping	Guilty	Life without parole
18.	1-23-48	J. Lescher	Sec. 209 Kidnapping	Guilty	Life without parole

3

The "Red Light Bandit"?

Was Caryl Chessman the "red light bandit"? This is the first question posed and the natural starting point for the inquiry. Indeed, the other three question areas all evolve from the true answer to this important question. This being said, it must immediately be added that no definitive answer exists as to the guilt of Chessman; and, at this late date, it is safe to say that none ever will. Chessman's twelve-year fight with the State of California muddied the track beyond any hope of finding a clear answer.

After spending a dozen years on Death Row and writing three self-aggrandizing books, Chessman possibly did not know the answer himself. He had been over his defense and denials so many times, savoring and perfecting the details in his imagination, that his grasp on reality is questionable. Any student of the Chessman affair who has read the final interviews he gave to Machlin and Woodfield, and to foreign writers such as the French journalist Dominique La Pierre, or the Spaniard Julio Camerero, will recognize the embellishments that occurred even in the few years since he wrote his wildly exaggerated autobiographical accounts of his criminal life. Except for one highly disputed confession shortly after his arrest, Chessman never wavered from his insistence of his innocence. If, indeed, he was the "red light bandit," as seems most probable to me, it would be the height of irony if he had succeeded in convincing himself of his innocence.

To question those victims of the "red light bandit" who are still alive would be a futile task. They have committed themselves to their identification of Chessman so often that, undoubtedly, his face is imprinted indelibly in their memory. Unquestionably, after the second or third time they were asked to identify Chessman, they were measuring their identification against the first time they saw Chessman—and not against the man who appeared at the door of their car. In their memory Chessman is that man at the door of the car. If some man came forth today with irrefutable proof that he was the true "red light bandit," it is most unlikely that any of these witnesses would believe it, no matter what proof was offered. Furthermore, most of the principals in the case are now dead. Since any new theory would have to be checked with the principals for accuracy, and this is impossible, the only way to arrive at a decision on the culpability of Chessman is from the evidence and statements that existed at the time of the trial. Little, if anything, that can be called real evidence has turned up since 1948.

If Chessman committed all the crimes for which he was charged, he had virtually no time to eat and sleep during the week commencing January 17, 1948. While that seems pretty unlikely on the face of it, the pre-1948 criminal record of Chessman does nothing to exclude the possibility of such a one-man crime wave. Judged by his past performances, he was well capable of such an effort.

When arrested as the "red light bandit" at the age of twenty-six, Chessman had already served the rather remarkable total of 113 months in California penal institutions of a juvenile or adult nature. To put it another way, from the time he reached the age of sixteen on May 27, 1937, until his "red light" arrest on January 23, 1948, Chessman had been out of penal custody only fifteen months. One of those months of freedom came when he escaped from Chino Correctional Institution, a minimum security prison near Los Angeles. Virtually all the others were a result of paroles from one correctional institution or another. His last time of freedom before the "red light" arrest lasted only forty-six days: He had been paroled from the maximum security Folsom State Prison on December 8, 1947. Clearly, Caryl Chessman was no angel.

A fair statement of the facts is that Chessman was a habitual, confirmed criminal. He was a small-time crook—holding up drugstores and filling stations, relieving bookmakers and whorehouse madams of the day's take, stealing cars—but this might have changed had he had more time to practice his trade. To all intents and purposes he never held a paying job, even after he married in mid-1940. He had no hesitation in trying to shoot his way out of situations where he might be arrested. In *Cell 2455, Death Row* he hinted that he had committed at least two murders, but as with everything else he said or wrote, one cannot be sure if he is telling the truth here.

But Chessman was not a typical criminal. He was obviously extremely intelligent—in I.Q. tests in reform school his scores had been very high—and he learned rapidly. Although he had not finished high school, he had a way with words and he wanted to be a writer. There is no question that this desire was authentic. At the time he was arrested in 1948 he had four completed manuscripts tucked away—*The Gladiator, The Disrobing Danseuse and L'Amour, Dust Thou Art,* and *Now Smoz Kapoz.* One of his alibis for the "red light" crimes was that he had been helping a friend who was trying to write a first novel. The four-plus books he wrote under difficult conditions in prison attest to the strength of his desire to write.

He also used his talents to sweet-talk the authorities. Look at the way the sixteen-year-old sought to convince the judge to place him on probation rather than send him to prison after he was convicted on his first felony, auto theft:

> This is my first time in Superior Court—my first time in felony tank—and I have been truly jolted. I now see crime in its true light, stripped of all its so-called glory. My last few months in jail have filled me with a strong revulsion against all things criminal,

including myself for having become ensnared in its brutal grip during my formative years. . . . Innately, I do not consider myself criminally inclined. From now on I plan to work, live simply, live properly.

His pleading got him off with a minimal road-gang sentence even though he already had a long, serious juvenile prison record. Released from custody, he hardly had changed his prison uniform before he was back at stealing cars. His high-sounding phrases of repentance were carefully filed away until the next time it was necessary to convince a judge that he was revolted by crime.

Again and again he persuasively promised to march forever after in the way of light and truth, and each time the authorities hoped that this time, finally, he meant it. But Chessman sang the same song too often. By 1948, California authorities could not have cared less what he had to say. This does not necessarily mean they treated Chessman unfairly. It does mean that they discarded, as totally unreliable, any statement he made about anything at all. And some of what Chessman later wrote in his autobiography, *Cell 2455, Death Row,* shows that the police were not entirely wrong to do this:

> Whit [i.e. Caryl Whittier Chessman] was arrested in the early morning hours of his seventeenth birthday. Two radio car officers spotted him in front of a Glendale, California, drugstore. Investigating, these officers found a crowbar and jimmie marks on the establishment's front door. Parked nearby was the postmaster's missing auto; at the police station Whit told one glib lie after another in accounting for his presence near the drugstore at that early hour of the morning. His conduct developed into a foolproof technique: tell near truths, half truths, but never the whole truth. Throw in a few outrageous fabrications and the police will give up in disgust. They'll become convinced you're a fraud and won't look too far.

Unless a criminal is caught at the scene of the crime with the stolen jewels or a smoking murder weapon in his hand, there can always be doubt that a defendant is guilty. Eyewitnesses can be mistaken; confessions can be coerced. For practical purposes there is no real metaphysical certainty of guilt. Thus it is not surprising that the experienced criminal almost automatically says, "It's a bum rap. I didn't do it." If that doesn't get the proper response, then in a voice straight out of an early Paul Muni or James Cagney movie he will moan: "I'm no good, Warden. I did them all. But not this one. Not the big one. You got to believe me, Warden. This time it's a bum rap." Chessman was both a clever and unrehabilitated criminal and, since he had a lot to lose if convicted, it is not surprising that he used these two lines again and again for the last twelve and one-half years of his life, from arrest to execution. When Caryl Chessman was paroled from Folsom on December 8, 1947, that by no means meant that the state of California had closed its books on him. One hundred sixty-one years of unserved time still remained over his head to be reimposed automatically if he were again convicted. When he was arrested on January 23, 1948, and charged with the "red light" crimes, he must have known that a conviction on even one of the more minor charges would imprison him for a long time. Even the more minor crimes, such as a stolen car or the housebreaking, were as large a threat to him as the more major robbery charges. It is not that a conviction would have, in reality, added 161 years to his sentence; that ostentatious figure was mostly window-dressing. California permits a man sentenced to life imprisonment with the possibility of parole to come before a parole board after only seven years. Thus, practically speaking, 161 years of unserved time undoubtedly meant ten to fifteen years. That is still nothing to sneeze at, especially when the sentence for any 1948 conviction was added on. No surprise Chessman decided to claim total innocence. In a nation where the Constitution says one must be regarded as innocent until proven guilty, and that one cannot be forced to incriminate himself, Chessman hardly can be blamed for this decision.

Given the serious position that Chessman would find himself in if convicted of any crime, the whole dispute about his alleged admission of guilt becomes more intelligible. This dispute could be totally cleared up only if we knew for sure at what point in the Chessman case the Los Angeles County District Attorney decided to go for the maximum sentence—the death penalty. Apparently, this did not happen until after Chessman admitted orally, but slightly ambiguously, culpability to some of the charges, including the grave attack on Mary Alice Meza; that is, he made an effort at plea bargaining. According to police, Chessman's admissions to them came before the D.A.'s office sent down the word—no deal. This timing is quite likely. Chessman, knowing the ropes, undoubtedly figured that if he pleaded guilty to some of the crimes, the state would go easy on the rest and recommend a lighter sentence. Plea bargaining of this type is tolerated by the courts because it saves much time and money. It is a dangerous tactic for a defendant; the state always has the upper hand. It won't promise anything until it hears what the defendant has to say. If it doesn't like what it hears, it simply says "no deal." However, the defendant's statement has been made freely and can be used against him.

Courts won't permit the prosecution to use this tactic to trap a defendant. If a skillful defense attorney is handling the bargaining, everything is kept in a hypothetical stage until the deal is made. One can surmise that Chessman neglected to keep things indefinite until the deal was made. However, he did not sign a confession and so one can guess he had some sense of how the system worked. But it was a bad tactical error on his part to give any indication of possible guilt in a case in which aggravated sexual attacks had occurred. Authorities are not likely to be generous in such a case. Chessman never denied that he made the admissions, but he always insisted that they were beaten from him.

With Chessman's criminal record before them, it was not difficult for the police to be convinced that Chessman was capable of committing the crimes in question. This made them receptive to believing the witnesses who identified Chessman as the "red light bandit." Because law enforcement authorities gave much credence to these identifications, during the trial the Prosecutor, J. Miller Leavy, went after the conviction of Chessman in an extremely vigorous manner and he built a good deal of his case on the identifications. Away from the pressures of the courtroom, it will be advantageous to examine the inherent reliability of these identifications. If they fall apart, it is impossible to say with certainty that Chessman committed these crimes.

Identifications are tricky. Many experts feel that there is no such thing as a reliable identification of a stranger. Earl Stanley Gardner, the top "whodunit" man of all time, once observed that eyewitness identifications are "just about the worst type of evidence." Many legal treatises have been written on the matter and the conclusion is generally the same: Eyewitness identifications are a most unreliable form of evidence and often cause miscarriage of justice. The reasons are obvious. As pointed out by John Henry Wigmore in the 1937 edition of his text, *The Science of Judicial Proof:*

> Most persons . . . have features not sharply distinctive of a few individuals (e.g. simply a large nose, blue eyes), and that most observers only receive the simplest impressions of features, expressible only in the loosest language (e.g. large nose, dark hair), it is easy to appreciate how often the items . . . as recorded, may be items common to many individuals, and yet may cause recognition of sameness.

Clearly, then, the identifications of Mrs. Johnson and the other nine people who identified Chessman must be regarded as inherently subject to suspicion. The most important question becomes not whether each identification was correct, but whether *all* of them were wrong. The question of police procedures in identifications will be taken up later, but now the question is whether eyewitness identifications provide any serious evidence that Chessman was the "red light bandit."

The most significant identifications were those related to Sec. 209 charges where the prosecution was asking for the death penalty: Regina Johnson, Mary Alice Meza, and the two men from the Redondo clothing store, Melvin Waisler, and Joe Lescher. The Meza identification was suspect because of her highly emotional state. The Redondo Beach identifications seemed reliable. The key identification, however, was that of Mrs. Johnson, the first prosecution witness. As discussed earlier, she does not seem to have been so upset that her judgement was affected. She had seen the assailant's face at close range and, despite her later hysteria, was positive it was Chessman. Hers was the testimony Chessman had to negate; he was never able to do so. It is my view that a reasonable man could have confidence that Mrs. Johnson and/or the Redondo Beach men were correct. Therefore, Chessman definitely should have been found guilty of at least some of the "red light crimes" and consequently returned to jail. This diminishes the relative importance of the less reliable identifications, except for the crucial question of the gas chamber.

It is interesting to note that, in later years, Chessman virtually ignored these identifications, especially that by Mrs. Johnson. When he talked of the unreliability of the identification, he concentrated on Mary Alice Meza's. Dominique La Pierre, a well-known French author who wrote *Chessman M'a Dit* after interviews with Chessman, apparently never heard of Mrs. Johnson. He had the impression that a Los Angeles prostitute jilted by Chessman was the other accuser besides Miss Meza. Incredibly, this information was attributed to the private detective who had worked seven years for Chessman. This would lead to the inference that, at least by 1960, the Chessman forces thought it was better to obscure the whole Johnson case in a shroud of untruths.

Alongside the identification question must be placed other facts and circumstances tending to indicate the guilt of Chessman. The most damning circumstances are those surrounding his capture. First of all, there was the whole melodramatic capture, complete with high speed chase. And then there is the fact that the Ford was stolen and contained all those incriminating items: a .45 pistol, a toy pistol, a pen-type flashlight, false license plates, the clothes, the money, and wallet from Redondo Beach.

The explanation Chessman attempted was fittingly elaborate. According to him, two other men originally were using the car; and, thus presumably, it was these other two who had been at Redondo Beach. On their way into Los Angeles, they picked up Chessman and, later, Knowles. The original driver of the car, later termed the "fourth man," left first. Chessman took over the driving and once in Los Angeles drove around a bit. Chessman maintains that before he spotted the police car of Riordan and May he pulled into the gas station so the "third man" could use the rest room. The third man got out. Knowles, like Chessman, was on parole, and it would be a parole violation for them to be found together. Thus, according to this account, Chessman fled at high speed to avoid the police who had driven into the service station behind them. Presumably the "third man" was left in the rest room. Knowles panicked and tried to grab the steering wheel from Chessman. This caused the car to crash.

In later years, Chessman alternated between hinting that the "red light bandit" was the man who got out of the car first, the "fourth man," and the man who got out at the gas station, the "third man." Chessman never seemed to make up his mind on this point. Policemen Riordan and May deny that anyone got out of the Ford at the gas station. They claim it drove straight through. Authorities also point out that the time it would have taken the "third" and "fourth" men to travel from Redondo Beach to Los Angeles after the robbery would have left little time to cruise around Los Angeles as Chessman described.

The conclusion appears inescapable that Chessman's story of the capture is total nonsense. He was caught cold with the evidence. One would think he would have had more sense than this. However, at least once before, he had driven a stolen car, taken from the local postmaster, for three days until he was captured at the end of a crime spree. But if the story is to be believed, it follows that he probably knew the identity of the true "red light bandit"— yet he refused to tell. Instead of trying to exculpate himself, he sat back and said, "I am innocent. Everyone is lying but me. I know who did it but won't squeal on another man. It is up to the cops to find the real 'red light bandit'." Given the other evidence against him, this approach was suicide.

In his various appeal petitions, his books or the interviews he gave, Chessman accused virtually everyone in sight of lying to him, lying about him, or persecuting him in some other manner because of their hatred of him. Officers Riordan and May lied about his arrest; Officers Forbes and Grant lied about his confession; Judge Fricke and Prosecutor Leavy lied about what went on at the trial; court reporter Fraser lied about the preparation of the trial manuscript; the wife of Governor Pat Brown and Cecil Poole, Brown's legal advisor and Clemency Secretary, both hated Chessman and talked the governor out of commuting his sentence to life imprisonment; two judges who held important hearings on the original trial transcript were charged with an un-rational hatred of him. At some point, the whole thing becomes absurd. When this point arrives, each individual charge of irregularity made by Chessman is, likewise, called into minute scrutiny.

This book has no intention of turning into an exegesis of the writings of Chessman. Pages could be wasted searching for hints about a third man in the Ford, or even a fourth man. The fictional names given by Chessman to characters in his autobiography could be examined for meaning. The continuity of his alibi could be traced. For anyone interested in exercises of this nature, *Ninth Life* by Machlin and Woodfield will give the reader more than his fill. The ridiculous length to which these men carried their speculations in my opinion demonstrates conclusively that it is impossible to operate under the assumption that Chessman was telling the truth. Every one of his statements must be taken with many grains of salt.

A few days before his execution, Chessman gave Dominique La Pierre the series of interviews that formed the basis for *Chessman M'a Dit*. La Pierre apparently bought, without hesitation, a tall tale of Chessman's, one which well illustrates his penchant for lying. Chessman emphasized that he had been framed by the police on the wishes of the Los Angeles criminal syndicate. Supposedly this was punishment for robbing syndicate bookmakers. Chessman said that the syndicate paid off the police and they arranged to frame him. This payoff became necessary only because Chessman had escaped from a group of gangsters who had been sent by the syndicate to kill him. He told La Pierre of being captured by these men who drove him into the desert. They took him to a high ridge and gave him a last cigarette to smoke before dispatching him to the afterworld. Chessman found a large rock near his foot. He picked it up, threw it at his captors, jumped forty feet into a ravine and escaped. Pretty good! Of course, it would be a little more believable if it had been in his autobiography written in 1954, six years earlier.

About the same time he talked to La Pierre, Chessman gave a number of interviews to Machlin and Woodfield. In *Ninth Life* they also recount a Chessman tale about some mystery in the desert, but this one is quite different from La Pierre's. This time it seems to have been the "fourth man" (the original driver of the

Ford, the one who left first) that was taken for a gangland ride, but he did not return. The phrasing is so ambiguous that it is even possible that this time Chessman was claiming he himself killed the "red-light bandit" in the desert. This is contrary to his claim that the fourth man left the Ford shortly after it returned to Los Angeles from Redondo Beach. No time existed for a gangland ride.

Machlin and Woodfield speculated that Chessman was silent to protect the identity and safety of an illegitimate daughter. Presumably this girl had been conceived in 1943 during the month that Chessman was on the loose as an escapee from Chino Honor Farm. The mother is unknown, although Chessman's autobiography mentions many women who could be possible candidates. Undoubtedly to try to heighten mystery and hinder those attempting to disprove his claims, Chessman never gave the true names of any of his companions in his autobiography. Machlin and Woodfield spent a lot of time on the story, frankly, more than seems warranted. They considered the possibilities for the mother, including a young woman who was briefly Chessman's wife. When they approached Chessman with their theory about protecting an illegitimate daughter, he dramatically said: "Let's not talk about that, shall we." Machlin and Woodfield interpreted this remark as confirmation of their theory. There was never any hint of an illegitimate daughter in the well-sketched picture of his life that Chessman provided in his books. To be candid, it seems a dubious story, totally out of keeping with Chessman's personality.

Though Chessman never gave an illegitimate daughter as a reason for not exposing the true "red light bandit," he did hint that fear for the safety of his parents kept his mouth sealed. Supposedly his father was threatened over the phone by the real bandit shortly after the trial. This story, too, seems out of character. Other than a lot of words in his books, one searches in vain for any proof of concern for his parents. His father was an unsuccessful businessman, habitually out of work. His mother, paralyzed from a 1929 auto accident, suffered constant pain, and by 1948 was mortally ill with cancer. Caryl, an only son, hardly ever earned a cent to ease the family's poverty, and of course he was in jail most of the time after he was sixteen. At the trial he had his mother carried into court on a stretcher to provide an alibi. The alibi was weak and it was cruel to subject her to such an ordeal; it probably lost him points with the jury. All of this makes it hard to believe that Chessman put his parents' interests before his own, especially when it meant the gas chamber.

Likewise, little faith can be attached to La Pierre's theory that "the code of the underworld" kept the lips of Chessman sealed, although it does give us a hint of the pseudoromantic image he liked to project. Somewhere or other he had read about François Villon, a fifteenth century French poet who was also a murderer and vagabond and whose poetry celebrated the life of the brigand and ridiculed the established authorities. Chessman was obsessed with Villon. He referred to him in his books over and over. One senses that Chessman wanted to emulate Villon's life, to rebel by robbery and murder but also by producing great literature. The image of Villon includes honoring the code of the underworld. At any rate, he solemnly assured La Pierre that this same code forced him to keep hidden the identity of the true bandit.

Perhaps Chessman thought people would see the Villon image in his statement soon after arrest that David Knowles was a good fellow and had not been in on the crime with him. Later, he backed off and denied making any such statement, except possibly during a beating. But this seems like hot air too. Knowles was caught in the Ford with him, less than two hours after the robbery. The clothes and the wallet were identifiable. The amount of money and types of guns present were consistent with the factual details of the robbery. More damagingly, the holdup men had not worn masks. They certainly would be identified the first time that their victims saw them. The claim that Chessman had committed it alone would quickly be exposed as patently fraudulent. In other words, Chessman was playing games; this was a grandstand attempt to take the blame for Knowles.

The importance that Chessman placed on his public image cannot be emphasized too strongly. The way he was captured was a great embarrassment to him. He could not picture the horsemen of the King of France ending the career of François Villon under such ignominious circumstances. Villon would have ridden off in a cloud of dust. Instead, Chessman was outrun in a footrace by a Los Angeles policeman. This is not the stuff of which legends are made. Later Chessman was to claim that May nicked him with a bullet, and that was the only reason he was captured. He cited as proof a scab on his forehead near the hairline. May denied that either of his warning shots touched Chessman. Since Chessman was not hurt, the detail is immaterial. Yet Chessman kept referring to this bullet constantly in his testimony, books, and legal documents. The only possible reason was that Chessman wanted to make sure everyone knew he was too speedy to be caught ordinarily.

Also, Chessman was disturbed that the police had outmaneuvered him in the car chase and forced him to bring his car to a crashing halt. This is not according to Chessman's script. To hear it from him, his great driving skill had enabled him to have the edge in the high-speed chase with the police. The stage was set for a superior piece of steering that would free him from his pursuers. At the crucial moment, his companion, Knowles, panicked and tried to grab the wheel. That caused Chessman to crash the car. By constantly talking about the car chase, he only emphasized that he was a danger to the community. At the trial, Chessman was responsive when the prosecutor questioned him at length on his driving skill. Each question brought forth a whole list of examples of other great driving feats he had performed in the past. The fact that describing these feats also entailed the description of a whole series of other crimes, many of which authorities were unaware of, did not deter him. The impact that this had on the jury can be imagined. Regardless of the fact that he was incriminating himself, he seemed compelled to convince all that he possessed extraordinary skills. What a high price he paid to be able to think of himself as the "second François Villon!"

If Chessman wasn't the "red light bandit," then who was? The Machlin-Woodfield team had a theory for this as well. They claimed that the culprit was Charles Terranova, a man who had been in jail with Chessman in 1948. Woodfield and Machlin thought he looked exactly like Chessman except for some key characteristics: He was shorter than Chessman, had protruding teeth and a scar above his right eyebrow, and looked Italian. He could have been the "third man," the one Chessman said got out at the gas station. The revelation was made just days before Chessman's execution in 1960. Terranova was hiding from the law on other charges and could not be questioned about the "red light" crimes, although the California statute of limitations would have protected him from prosecution for those crimes in 1960. Machlin and Woodfield were upset that the police had not questioned Terranova earlier.

The theory simply does not hold up. Even after the announcement, with his execution looming just days away, Chessman had little to say one way or the other about the charge that Terranova and not he was guilty of the "red light" crimes. The whole story rests on the notion of the "third man," but the sworn testimony of the policemen was that no one got out at the gas station. As Machlin and Woodfield later presented and expanded on the theory in *Ninth Life*, it appeared to contradict their version of the mysterious ride in the desert in which the "fourth man" was really the "red light bandit." The stress on Terranova's resemblance to Chessman is over done. So is the argument that Terranova was aggressive sexually, an assertion which rests on a statement by Terranova's wife that he had tried to rape her on the first date. All in all, the evidence is shallow and the theory as bizarre as a lot of others in *Ninth Life*.

In sum, not one shred of evidence exists that anyone other than Chessman was the "red light bandit." Only the height discrepancy should have given cause for doubt. Interestingly, early reports by both Regina Johnson and Mary Alice Meza raised the possibility that a second person was crouched down in the back seat of the Ford. However, as in the case of Mary Alice, where did this second man go when she was forced to get in the back seat? If there were a second, smaller man, this would not exonerate Chessman. His involvement in all phases of the crime would make him an accomplice equally responsible for legal punishment. However, it is just as hard to visualize Chessman hiding in the back and playing a secondary role, as it is to visualize him keeping quiet and allowing someone else to get off scott free while he was executed for their crimes.

Sensation-seeking writers notwithstanding, the conclusion from this examination is that Caryl Chessman was the "red light bandit." However, reaching this conclusion is just the first step. Even though he had committed these crimes he still had to be proven guilty beyond a reasonable doubt at a fair trial. If this was not done, then in our form of government he had as much right to walk the streets as you or I. The next section will examine his trial.

4

The Trial:
Chessman for the
Defense

The case of the People of the State of California against Caryl Whittier Chessman began April 4, 1948. While the conduct of the trial is questionable in several respects, it is necessary to remember that it took place a quarter of a century ago. Harry S. Truman was president, Al Zarilla, Gene Bearden, and Bruce Edwards were among the top baseball players of the day. Not one man in a hundred had yet heard of Korea, or thought of men walking on the moon. The generation of "flower children" and peace marchers was not yet born. By our present standards of justice, it is easy to be horrified at what took place in the Chessman trial. But we cannot expect 1948 people to live by 1975 standards of experience, knowledge, and intelligence. The important question is whether or not Chessman received a fair trial by the standards of his day, not by the standards of our day.

Why is it wrong to condemn past trials if they do not accord to present-day standards? The main reason is that the police were also acting by 1948 standards. Laws and the day-by-day application of them change in relation to the social, political, economic, geographic, and religious realities of any particular period. The rough and ready justice of the days of the California gold rush would have been most out of place 100 years later. To a lesser degree, our whole lifestyle has changed since 1948, demanding a completely different application of our laws. As the laws and their applications change, the enforcers of the law will change their practices to keep up with them. If the laws and practices of 1948 were observed, Chessman received a fair trial by 1948 standards.

It may very well be that the laws of 1948 were weighted against the defendant. The liberal decisions by the United States Supreme Court that vastly expanded the rights of defendants were still far in the future. However, if the criminal laws were stacked against defendants in those days, this status applied to all defendants and not to Chessman alone. The balance and emphasis between the rights of individuals and the rights of society as a whole, never have and never will be in exact harmony. This indicates that justice is not perfect. It does not indicate that each trial is so unfairly weighted in favor of either the defendant or society as a class, that one can say justice will never be done. Imperfect people will render justice in an imperfect fashion. The only group in our history able to claim that all trials in which they were forced to partake were fundamentally unfair are the Southern blacks, forced to stand in a Deep South state court for a crime against a white man.

Now we must turn to the trial, held in the spring of 1948. Chessman insisted on being his own attorney, both at the preliminary hearing and at the trial itself. He firmly turned down the services of the Public Defender assigned to him. It is beyond argument that the whole trial would have been conducted in a very different manner if Chessman had not bullheadedly insisted on being his own attorney. Unless a defendant is either insane or utterly incapable of conducting his own defense, his sixth-amendment rights as a citizen allow him to be a damned fool if he insists. Chessman exercised this prerogative.

At the preliminary hearing, forty-eight days before the start of the actual trial, the following dialogue took place. The judge was Arthur S. Guerin:

THE COURT: Are you a good lawyer?

THE DEFENDANT CHESSMAN: I think so.

THE COURT: Few lawyers say they are good.

THE DEFENDANT CHESSMAN: I think I am a good enough lawyer.

THE COURT: You don't want to trust it to a lawyer?

THE DEFENDANT CHESSMAN: I don't want to do it.

THE COURT: What will probably happen, if we set this case down for trial, you will want a lawyer and then ask for a continuance. If you want to try your own case, there is no way that we can tell you not to. You will have to try it or have someone hired to represent you in plenty of time to try the case at the time it is set.

THE DEFENDANT CHESSMAN: I understand that.

THE COURT: Because many times men with past experience such as you have had—you know the tricks of the trade, and they get a lawyer at the very last minute. You really want to try your own case?

THE DEFENDANT CHESSMAN: That is correct.

Prior to the day his trial began, Chessman talked with six different lawyers. He actually hired and quickly fired three. Sometimes the point in disagreement was the fee; other times it was a question of trial tactics. It appears that finally Chessman had decided to be represented by William Ives. Chessman's father was to borrow the funds. A sudden illness of the father made this impossible. After this, Chessman decided to stand alone.

The newspapers tagged him as "the criminal genius." Naturally, Chessman loved this nickname and tried to live up to it. He was convinced that he could understand everything that he read and, consequently, he could be a great lawyer because he was a fast talker and a shrewd questioner. Later he summed up his own opinion of his decision well in *Cell 2455, Death Row:*

> I needed an inspired advocate—an Erskine, a Pruiett, a Darrow, a Fallon, a Rogers and a Liebowitz all in one—an unconquerable, dynamic legal gladiator eager and willing to punch gaping holes in the prosecutor's case. I needed a dedicated champion willing to fight for me every inch of the way through the trial. That was

what I needed and I ended up with a fool for a client. I decided to represent myself.

But even after writing this, Chessman insisted on running his own defense during the many appeals and hearings that followed his trial. During his twelve-year fight to stay alive, he hired, fought with, and fired, a whole host of competent attorneys. There is no getting away from the fact that he refused to share the spotlight. But even if he had possessed an adequate knowledge of law, his abrasive personality and emotional tirades against those who opposed him indicate that he should have left the task to others.

The written appeals of Chessman displayed arrogance, lack of tact, impetuousness, and a lack of fundamental legal grounding. One example should illustrate this point: In one of his arguments to the California Supreme Court he claimed that they were not legally qualified to review his or any case because they did not reside and keep offices in Sacramento as required in some Government Code that he had read.

Judicially, the objection was questionable; tactically, it was most imprudent. The objection had little chance of being granted. It only confirmed the California Supreme Court Justices in their opinion that Chessman was playing games, and must have affected their judgment when dealing with his more serious claims. To the very last moment of his short life, Chessman was his own worst enemy.

The first mistake that Chessman made at the 1948 trial came on the first day of his trial. In a colossal tactical error from which he never recovered, he willingly settled for, even actively solicited, a jury of eleven women and only one man. Four of these women had teen-age daughters and one had a son who was a Los Angeles policeman. If one in advance tried to imagine the worst jury possible for Chessman, the actual result could not have been surpassed. It is virtually inevitable that the four mothers (like Mrs. Johnson) of the teen-age daughters (like Mary Alice Meza) would identify with these two women. The result would certainly be unfavorable for Chessman.

During the trial Chessman missed so many chances to object to improper procedures or evidence that reviewing courts decided this was a tactic to goad the prosecution and judge into a mistrial. The appellate courts seem to discount errors in the trial, saying that even a nonlawyer like Chessman should have known enough to object. The only explanation they find for this was a deliberate effort to pervert justice. Thus, the California Supreme Court held that Chessman had forfeited the right to make the objections at a later time, even though they went to the heart of fundamental fairness. This reasoning was, at best, highly questionable. Still, it demonstrates again that Chessman would have been far wiser to hire an attorney who would not have let these errors slip by without objecting and receiving a ruling from the judge. The judge in the case, Charles W. Fricke, advised Chessman when he insisted on defending himself: "I have been in this business practicing law for pretty near forty-five years, and if I found myself in the position in which you are, I would hire a good lawyer."

Why did Chessman choose to defend himself? In addition to the obvious fact that he thought of himself as a mental hotshot, he always claimed that he could not afford a good lawyer and that he was better than all but the best. It is true that his parents had little money; whether Chessman had any is unknown. Actually often the best attorneys are not as expensive as the more flashy, specimens. Chessman certainly could have found a good criminal attorney had he looked. But the evidence seems pretty clear that he didn't want an attorney.

In 1948, California had an excellent public defender system, far ahead of most other states in providing a state-paid system of advocates for indigent prisoners. These men were in court each day and had great experience in criminal trials. They automatically would have cut down on the errors that the legal novice, Chessman, committed. Chessman did use the services of Al Matthews, an assistant public defender, as a legal adviser. This meant Matthews could sit next to Chessman and make suggestions, but not actually try the case for him. Certainly Matthews must have told him how unwise it was to have eleven women on the jury. The conclusion is inescapable that Chessman never listened to him. Even after Chessman had obtained enough money from his best-selling books to hire top-flight attorneys such as George T. Davis, Ben Rice, and Abe Wirin, he often failed to listen to them either. Under these circumstances, one cannot shift the blame to Matthews for defense mistakes during the original trial.

Even Chessman's strongest attribute, his ability in using words, turned out to be his enemy when he started to play lawyer. His cross-examining method was not appreciated by the jury. It was not that he lacked skill in his area—just the opposite. He was too sharp, too persistent. The same man charged with attacking two women and robbing a whole score of other people was again committing assault; this time, only with words, but the thought undoubtedly played on the minds of the jurors. The tricky, argumentative jailhouse-lawyer style of Chessman did not win him any points either. His whole attitude was such as to cast grave doubts on the sincerity with which he denied guilt.

By defending himself, Chessman brought his own personality into the case to a degree in which it would not otherwise have been present. If Chessman had been represented by an attorney, the victims would have been cross-examined by an intermediary. This automatically would have removed a great deal of sting from their answers. It is a different matter to be told you are mistaken by a lawyer who presumably is questioning you politely and intelligently, than it is to be told so by the man you are certain actually attacked you. If Chessman had been represented by an attorney, Mrs. Johnson could not have replied to questions in the same manner as she did to Chessman. She hurt his case mightily in this fashion. Each time Chessman asked her what the attacker did next, she would reply, "next you did. . . ." This, of course, stuck the knife a little deeper into Chessman. He did no better with Mary Alice Meza. Chessman at first seemed to be poking a large hole in her story on the height question. He got her to admit that she had originally described the height of her attacker as being only slightly more than her own five-feet five-inches. He then called attention to his own six-foot stature. She looked him straight in the face and said, "I know it was you." This sort of dramatic, stunning direct rebuttal of Chessman's story would not have been possible if he had employed an attorney as an intermediary between him and the witnesses.

Defense Counsel Chessman's antagonist was Prosecutor J. Miller Leavy, and the judge in the case was Charles W. Fricke. As fate would have it, both had major roles in the Barbara Graham murder trial in 1954. The point is important because both the Chessman and the Graham cases had an extraordinary dimension of publicity and were linked together as examples of injustice in California. Barbara Graham was convicted as one of the three murderers of Mabel Monahan, an elderly widow of an underworld figure who was robbed and beaten to death with a gun in 1954. Only the third woman to die in San Quentin's gas chamber, Graham was executed in 1955. Her last night was spent in the Death Row holding chamber, only a few feet away from the others on the Row, including Chessman. Before and after her execution, there were allegations that she had been framed, and this was hinted in the movie which made the case famous, "I Want to Live." The allegations sounded like the complaints of the still-alive Chessman, who had managed in 1954 to smuggle *Cell 2455, Death Row* out of the jail and get it published. The authorities were quick to label him another Barbara Graham. They tended to take out their frustration at being portrayed as villians in the Graham case by tightening the screws even more on Chessman.

In 1960 there was an even more specific connection between the Graham and Chessman cases. In a special legislative hearing on a proposal to abolish capital punishment in California, a proposal arising directly out of the Chessman case, J. Miller Leavy testified that Barbara Graham had confessed to her part in the Monahan murder. Supposedly she had confessed to the San Quentin Warden, Harley Teets. Teets, who was dead by this time, made no official record of this, but the claim was that he did tell William Weissich, Marin County District Attorney, who told Leavy. The most significant aspect of Leavy's revelation of a Graham confession was the way it affected Chessman's fight for his life. First of all, it probably had a lot to do with the legislature's decision to pigeonhole the proposal to abolish the death penalty. Moreover, if Graham, who had claimed she was framed and fought execution, had actually been guilty and had confessed, then her case was not an example of a miscarriage of justice. The implication was that Chessman was also guilty and would confess before execution. He did no such thing. The quiet dignity with which he went to his death, "like a man and not an animal" as he expressed it, was in total contradiction to most of his nihilistic life.

5

Prosecutor Leavy

The role of the prosecutor in a criminal case is not hard to define: he is an agent of justice. Take, for instance, the following paragraph from a 1935 United States Supreme Court decision. The prosecutor in question was the United States Attorney; however, the standard of conduct as defined applies just as well to our state court system:

> The United States Attorney is the representative not of an ordinary party to a controversy 'but of a sovereignty whose obligation to govern is as compelling as its obligation to govern at all; and whose interest, therefore, in a criminal prosecution is not that it shall win a case, but that justice shall be done. As such, he is in a peculiar and very definite sense the servant of the law, the two-fold aim of which it is that guilt shall not escape or innocence suffer. He may prosecute with earnestness and vigor—indeed he should do so. But while he may strike hard blows, he is not at liberty to strike foul ones. It is as much his duty to refrain from improper methods calculated to produce a wrongful conviction as it is to use every legitimate means to bring about a just one. (*Berger* v. *United States,* 295 U.S. 78 [1935].)

Everything said by the Supreme Court about the role of a prosecutor is true. But how easy it is for a United States Supreme Court Justice to sit in the splendid isolation of his panelled office and write such an ode to justice. What a difference from the noisy crowded courtrooms of the Los Angeles Hall of Justice; there it is that overworked prosecutors struggle to forge a rough idea of justice, that at least to some extent the people are protected. In a large number of cases they can act in the manner sanctified by the United States Supreme Court, safe in the knowledge that they have done their duty and protected the citizen. But Caryl Chessman's case was not like this.

In many ways, Chessman was the forerunner of Abbie Hoffman, Bobby Seale, George Jackson, the defendant who refuses to play by the rules. Look again at the definition of the duties of a prosecutor. What does it forget? Precisely the Chessman-type case where the defendant will not play by the rules. The prosecutor is enjoined "from improper methods calculated to produce a wrongful conviction." What about the case in which he feels it necessary to use improper means to obtain a conviction he believes just? This is a central dilemma of our legal system. The people are not protected unless the guilty are punished.

As a public official charged with seeing that criminals are placed behind bars, the prosecutor fails if a truly guilty man is acquitted. If the prosecutor plays by the rules in trying to convict and the jury makes the mistake of acquitting, that is one of the prices of our system of justice. But it upsets some people especially when they feel that the defendant manipulated the law to evade justice, but the prosecution let its hands be tied by the law. They ask which is worse, relatively speaking, criminals walking the streets because they manipulated our legal system or prosecutors willing to bend the law to get a just result?

The role of a prosecutor in any case is a source of contradiction. A prosecutor is the protector of the rights of the people. However, the defendant is one of these people to whom he owes an obligation. The prosecutor can rationalize this difficulty by saying that he only presents the evidence and leaves it up to the jury to decide. This response has truth in it but it ignores the human desire to win in any combat in which one finds himself engaged. It also forgets that a prosecutor is under pressure from superiors and the public to obtain convictions. Judgment on the conduct of the prosecutor at Chessman's trial cannot be fairly abstracted from judgments on the whole fundamental fairness of our criminal judicial system in this country.

The prosecutor, J. Miller Leavy, was a Deputy District Attorney with a lot of experience in criminal trials. He acted at all times as if Chessman was using dishonest means as he tried to prove his innocence. Leavy clearly was deeply convinced of Chessman's guilt. It would be an overstatement to say that Leavy felt it necessary to use illegal means to obtain the just conviction of Chessman. But it can be said that he pushed very hard. The crimes in question were clearly repugnant to him. Both Mrs. Johnson and Miss Meza evoked, and got from Leavy, a great deal of sympathy. Chessman was a slick, flamboyant, and exasperating defense attorney. Because Leavy believed Chessman was definitely the "red light bandit," and because Leavy thought that Chessman was trying to razzle-dazzle his way out of a just conviction, he leaned extra hard on Chessman.

In all respects, Prosecutor Leavy displayed a true killer's instinct. His prosecutorial style could have been out of a movie or a TV show. He was shrewd, unrelenting, quick, bullying, and insinuating. He asked questions "not to learn but to convict," in the phrase of John Mason Brown. His behavior was appropriate to the essential flavor of any well-fought criminal trial. It is a life and death combat. The motives are the same as a championship prize fight. The appellate courts which later chided Leavy's conduct forgot this reality. It is not to excuse Leavy for prosecutorial excesses. It is an attempt to situate them within the true context of the everyday reality of the trial of a major criminal case. To point to specific statements of the Prosecutor that were excessive is not hard. An example is his manipulation of the facts of Mrs. Johnson's bout with polio, suggesting she had recovered from the illness just before the attack. Also, Leavy attacked the veracity of the character witnesses of Chessman beyond all bounds of propriety. He objected to certain technical pieces of evidence in Chessman's favor that he should have allowed to be admitted without objection. He drummed into the jury that any sentence less than death bore the possibility that a later parole, pardon, or change of law could put Chessman back on the streets—a free man.

As the California Supreme Court pointed out, a lot of these excesses would have been checked if Chessman had objected. The judge would have ruled in favor of Chessman and ameliorated the excessive zeal of Leavy. Chessman did nothing. No check was placed on Leavy; no corrective to his conduct appeared in the record because Chessman never asked for one. Chessman supporters have tried to make Leavy a central villain of the piece. But Leavy should not be seen as the villain. He was a skillful prosecutor who played his role properly in terms of how our system really works, who believed in his cause, and who thought he was serving justice.

6

Judge Fricke

The third figure of importance in the trial was Judge Charles W. Fricke. Aggressive as were Chessman and Leavy, neither had anything on him. Fricke had been a judge on the criminal side of the Superior Court in Los Angeles since 1927. He had been a prosecutor in California and Wisconsin before that. He was a legal scholar of note and his courtroom reputation was of being fair. But his sentences were harsh. He had sentenced more men to death than any judge in the history of California. This may be more of a testimonial to the amount of crime in Los Angeles during the twenties and thirties than to bloodthirstiness on his part, but his nickname, "San Quentin Charlie," should not be forgotten in our discussion of the Chessman trial.

As the title Judge signifies, seeing that justice is done is his function. What this means concretely is difficult to say. As close as anyone has come is the following comment by Chief Justice Weintraub of the New Jersey Supreme Court:

> Truth and justice are inseparable. A deliberately false judgment debases the judicial process, and no less so because the false judgment is an acquittal. . . . The first right of an individual is to

be protected from attack. That is why we have government, as the preamble to the Federal Constitution plainly says. In the words of *Chicago* v. *Sturges,* 222 U.S. 313, 322, 56 L. Ed. 215, 220 (1911): "Primarily government exists for the maintenance of social order. Hence it is that the obligation of the government to protect life, liberty and property against the conduct of the indifferent, the careless, and the evil-minded, may be regarded as lying at the very foundation of the social compact."

To facilitate the orderly working of this most fundamental task of society, a judge is present to guard both the rights of the people and of citizen-defendant during the trial process. There can be no argument that Charles Fricke tried to do this in the Chessman case. But the pugnacious attitude of Chessman seemed to irritate Fricke and he clearly was not at ease. "What is he going to try next?" seemed always to be going through the judge's mind. Clearly, in this mood he could not be impartial. It was an impossible situation for any judge. Not only was Chessman's courtroom conduct extraordinary, but Leavy was constantly making verbal knife swipes at Chessman's jugular vein. Even Solomon could not have kept peace between these protagonists.

Fricke was by no stretch of the imagination another Solomon; his leanings were in favor of the police. This did not make him unique. In fact, it was common in states such as California where selection to the Superior Court was by election. Only those who received nomination from political bosses stood a chance of winning. Service to the party and to the city in the district attorney's office was virtually the only way to win political support for a judicial election. This bred an unhealthy alliance between judiciary and local government. If Fricke tended to lean toward the government in his decisions, he was only mirroring the common state of affairs in large American cities. There is not a question of payoffs or conscious unjust decisions. However, a man who came through the law enforcement ranks to the judiciary understandably would have a favorable attitude toward law enforcement in general. A judge from this type of background must constantly remind himself that the defendant is innocent until proven guilty. He cannot let himself think, "I know the district attorney; he would not bring this fellow into court if he were not pretty sure he were guilty."

Although Judge Fricke's attitudes may be described as law and order attitudes, he was a long way from being a political hack. He was not the local ward politician. He was a prolific writer and a legal scholar of note. Many important textbooks on criminal law in California carry his name: *California Criminal Law*, six editions; *California Criminal Evidence*, four editions; *California Criminal Procedure*, four editions; *California Peace Officers Manual*, nine editions; *Planning and Trying Cases*, two editions; *5000 Criminal Definitions, Terms and Phrases*, five editions; *Sentence and Probation: The Imposition of Penalties Upon Convicted Criminals.*

In many ways, a legal scholar was the worst possible type of judge for the Chessman case. Because this defendant insisted on defending himself, there was an absolute guarantee that the model defense of a criminal case as prescribed in Fricke's own work, *Planning and Trying Cases*, was going to be conspicuously absent in the courtroom. Fricke knew California law and he appeared grimly determined to insist that Chessman observe every aspect of it. Legal formalities were observed with harsh rigor throughout the trial.

It did not take Leavy, the experienced prosecutor, long to figure things out. He objected at the slightest deviation from proper procedure. Many of the technical objections concerned procedures only known to attorneys, and not to all of them. Chessman was not listening to his legal advisor, and so was hurt by many technical points of law that he could not conceivably know. Anyone less bullheaded than Chessman would have given up and hired an attorney. Because he did not do so, he was constantly ruled against on trivial matters that he did not understand. As a consequence, he became upset and as his frustration mounted, his behavior became even more outrageous. This led to even more objections by Leavy, sustained by Fricke, who repeatedly told Chessman, "I am not here to conduct a law school course."

A few small hints to Chessman and a less firm hand on the tiller would have gone a long way toward establishing an atmosphere conducive to deciding guilt or innocence without the complicating factor of emotionalism. Judge Fricke failed to establish such an atmosphere. It is entirely possible that no one could have established such an atmosphere in dealings with the mercurial Chessman. But it is certain that Judge Fricke did not try very hard. He warned Chessman about the danger of attempting to conduct his own defense. When this failed, he washed his hands of the whole affair. The fairness of this in a possible death penalty case is highly questionable.

We are faced with an unusual situation. Often a judge leans over too far to assist a defendant proceeding without legal counsel. A Federal Circuit Court of Appeals opinion pointed out that a judge is not expected to act as the defendant's attorney:

> When appellant chose to proceed without counsel, he chose a course of action fraught with the danger that he would commit legal blunders. But having made that choice he did not thereby acquire the right to have the court act as his counsel whenever he seemed to be blundering. It cannot be said that the court denied him representation of counsel, or denied him a fair trial because the judge refrained from intermeddling.

If intermeddling occurred in the Chessman case, it was not in any attempt to assist the defendant who was representing himself. The intent would appear to have been just the opposite.

Even though it is unquestionable that Judge Fricke did not bend over backwards to help Chessman, that is a long way from prejudicial conduct justifying a reversal. Fricke clearly emphasized to the jury that it was the burden of the state to prove the defendant guilty beyond a reasonable doubt. What Fricke seems to have done was to assume that Chessman, though innocent until proven guilty, would do everything in his power, regardless of its legality, to prevent the state from completing its task. This brings us right back to the situation that, because Chessman seemed prepared to throw out the rule book, everyone else followed suit.

What happened was that an encyclopedic legal brain worked at full speed to block the slightest advantage from swinging the way of the defendant. In most trials inconsequential errors favoring the prosecution or defense tend to even out. But because of the vigilance of Fricke, this never happened in the Chessman case; he pounced on all of Chessman's many errors.

This meant about three times the normal number of breaks fell Leavy's way, causing a striking disparity. This rare set of circumstances conceivably constituted grounds for a reversal in itself.

Judge Fricke refused to allow Chessman a continuance in order to try to raise the money to pay the attorney, Ives, when the elder Chessman could not borrow the money. But judicial strictness in dealing with Chessman had begun long before Fricke got the case. When Judge Guerin told Chessman that he would have to hire an attorney long enough before the trial so that the man would be ready to start on the appointed date, his warning was unusual. It emphasized the special attention accorded Chessman. Fricke's insistence in following suit reinforced the special nature of the case. Virtually no attention seemed to be paid to the fact that Chessman was on trial for his life. It is true that Chessman might have gotten into a dispute with Ives during the postponement and have fired him also, and then requested still another continuance to find another lawyer. But it would seem that a short delay could have been granted without compromising the search for truth. Fricke had granted one brief continuance when he allowed Chessman's motion to have his trial separated from that of Knowles. It's too bad he did not allow another.

When Chessman decided to defend himself, he may have thought of himself as another Perry Mason, but the Sheriff of Los Angeles County insisted on treating him as just another accused criminal who remained in his custody because he could not come up with bail. Chessman was not allowed to leave his cell to interview witnesses. He was not given the law books that he requested for his instruction. He was not allowed to use a typewriter with which to make legal motions. An appeal to Judge Fricke for relief from these harsh conditions met with no success at all. More could and should have been done to allow Chessman to prepare his defense. Sometimes one would think from the attitude of the authorities that they were dealing with a penny-candy store robbery with a maximum penalty of ten days or $10. The whole attitude of Fricke was to allow Chessman to stew in his own juice. Although one can overdo the criticism of Fricke for his lack of sympathy for Chessman, his refusal to be of any assistance to Chessman, even when the defendant requested the proper form to pose a tricky question so that it would be acceptable in evidence, seems excessive.

At the start of the trial, it became clear that Judge Fricke had already made some decisions about how to conduct it. On his own initiative, he informed Chessman that he must conduct his defense from his place at the defendant's table. He could stand when addressing the court, witnesses, or jurors. However, he could not move closer to any of these people. Leavy, a master of courtroom tactics, was under no such restraint. He was free to get right under the nose of a difficult witness, and sidle up to a sympathetic juror during argument. He could walk away from a witness to emphasize tension or disgust or merely to relieve boredom. All these normal courtroom tactics were denied Chessman. He was forced to remain riveted to his spot and address all remarks literally half the length of the courtroom. During long questioning, this must have become tiring and nerve-racking for Chessman, and boring for the jury. Any lawyer would have difficulty adequately presenting his case under circumstances such as these. To require a nonlawyer on trial for his life to operate under such circumstances is to impose a serious burden.

Apparently, Fricke feared Chessman might attempt to escape and this caused him to be so severe in the limitations he imposed on the defendant. Chessman had a history of escapes under dramatic circumstances. After his first arrest, on his sixteenth birthday, he escaped from police (during a medical examination prior to booking) by jumping out an open window and was not recaptured until 3:30 the next morning. And there are many examples of violence, escape, kidnapping, and even murder occurring in a courtroom, most recently in the dramatic 1969 Marin County shootout leading to the Angela Davis trial. In *Cell 2455, Death Row*, Chessman admitted he considered trying to break out of Fricke's courtroom. But what is disturbing is that the judge never gave Chessman a chance to operate under ordinary rules of movement before clamping on these heavy restrictions. A stiff warning of what would happen at the first signs of monkey business would seem to be much fairer when a man is trying to conduct his own defense so as to evade the gas chamber.

Appellate courts never commented on the fact that Chessman was not even given a chance to operate in a normal manner, depending upon his continuing good conduct. The right of a trial judge to regulate conduct in his own courtroom was emphasized by the appellate court when reviewing the propriety of this action by Fricke. Even more disturbingly, the California Supreme Court indulged in some highly questionable theorizing concerning the legal status of a defendant who chooses to try his own case. "In representing himself he retained this status (prisoner) and did not attain that of an attorney at law who is an officer of the court and responsible to it." There is a question as to whether the customary prerogatives of defense attorneys in criminal cases can be stripped away from a man exercising his constitutional right to defend himself, merely because he is not a member of the bar. The danger in this regard is well stated by Mr. Justice Felix Frankfurter in a 1942 opinion:

> The right to assistance of counsel and the correlative right to dispense with a lawyer's help are not legal formalisms, they rest on considerations that go to the substance of an accused's position before the law. The public conscience must be satisfied that fairness dominates the administration of justice. An accused must have the means of presenting his best defense. He must have time and facilities for the investigation and for the production of evidence. But evidence and truth are of no avail unless they can be adequately presented. Essential fairness is lacking if an accused cannot put his case effectively in court. But the Constitution does not force a lawyer upon a defendant. He may waive his constitutional right to assistance of counsel if he knows what he is doing and his choice is made with eyes open.

But, in fact, Chessman seems to have had his eyes open all along. If he had decided to defend himself before he knew that the judge would restrict his conduct, the argument could be raised that Chessman had waived his right to legal representation without being aware of all the ramifications of that decision. Chessman dispelled any thoughts along this line when he said, as quoted in the transcript: "I wish to point out that it is my intention to act in *propria persona* at this time and to continue to do so until such time as it is legally established that I am not qualified to do so, and that I will not accept a court-appointed attorney."

But even if his eyes were open, there is a serious question as to whether the jury might have been prejudiced because of the restrictions placed on his movements at the trial. Chessman never raised this point in any of his appeals, although he did claim that the restraints hampered him in his conduct of his defense. However, simply because Chessman never thought to question the possible prejudice that might have occurred because of the restrictions does not mean that prejudice did not occur. It might have implied to the jury, "See! We are so afraid of Chessman that we won't let him walk around this courtroom. Why, he might attack one of you nice ladies on the jury!" A perceptive appellate court should have taken notice of the possible prejudice due to the restrictions on movement placed upon the accused defending himself, even though Chessman did not raise the issue. But this was not done. Too often in this case, the appellate courts seemed more interested in backing up the home team than in making a thorough, impartial search to ascertain whether justice was done at the trial. In my view, the movement restrictions did not constitute a major error that, alone, would demand a reversal. However, it is an element that should have been weighed in the overall decision as to whether enough error was present to demand a reversal of the conviction. It is most doubtful that it was considered at all. Instead, this subject must be assigned to the large group of seemingly minor incidents that were not handled in the manner that we expect from American justice.

The most disputed aspect of all the trial materialized from a seemingly minor incident. Early in the trial, Caryl Chessman requested that the courtroom reporter, Ernest Perry, type up the trial transcript daily and make it available to him and the prosecution. Judge Fricke refused. There does not appear to be any logical reason for refusing this request. All this entailed was the courtroom stenographer translating his symbols into English and typing the translation. Clearly the trial was going to be long and bitterly contested. Both sides would have many occasions to refer to previous testimony. The easiest way to forestall arguments as to what had been said would be to refer to an exact transcription.

In later years, Fricke never gave a satisfactory explanation for his denial of the request for a daily transcript. He stated that the prosecutor did not join in the request with Chessman. However, legal scholar that he was, Fricke was quick to add that he still could have granted the request; there was no legal requirement that the prosecutor join in the request. In fact, Leavy says Fricke never asked him. Besides, an experienced judge like Fricke would be aware that a prosecutor has no trouble getting the court reporter to type up any part of the shorthand notes that he needs. Prosecutors and courtroom reporters have been together on many cases. Slight favors passing between them are common occurrences. Also, all courtroom reporters are court appointees and incurring wrath of the prosecutors is not a recommended way to keep in the good graces of the court, and thereby, stay on the county payroll. All in all, there is no question that Leavy could have arranged, albeit unofficially, to read any of the past testimony which interested him. Thanks to the ruling of the judge, Chessman was denied this privilege. Fricke could not remember ever denying any defendant such a request in any other long criminal trial in which he presided. The conclusion is inescapable that Fricke denied the request because of his attitude toward Chessman. Any lawyer representing Chessman would not have allowed this to happen. Chessman, obviously bewildered, just shrugged his shoulders and said nothing.

Trial transcripts are an extremely difficult, often litigated element of criminal law. The record of what actually happened at the trial is of crucial importance whenever there is an appeal from a conviction. It is not our purpose to examine this intricate subject at any length here. The bizarre history of the Chessman trial transcript will be examined later in this book at great length. The point is to demonstrate the rigidity of Judge Fricke. True, he could not have known that this action' would have such great consequences. This does not excuse him. There is nothing to gain by denying a daily record to Chessman except for a relatively small outlay on overtime pay to a court reporter.

Had Judge Fricke granted the request for a daily transcription, the Chessman affair as we know it never would have occurred. Without the disputed trial transcript, Chessman never would have been able to keep his appeals going for twelve years. He probably would have reached his fate six or seven years sooner. Ironically, it is not at all sure that this fate would have been the gas chamber. Without a red-hot issue on which to castigate the court system, the thoroughly obnoxious personality of Chessman would not have been so nakedly exposed. If his appeal had been more routine, it probably would have received little attention. The fact that he had not killed anyone or caused physical mutilation would have weighed in his favor. Unquestionably his conviction would not have been overturned; but it is quite possible, even probable, that his death sentence would have been commuted to life imprisonment, as was the case with one third of California prisoners sentenced to death between 1943 and 1957. In that fifteen-year period only one nonmurderer was gassed. The refusal of the request to transcribe the notes of the reporter on a daily basis did no one any good—neither Chessman nor the criminal justice system of the State of California.

It is hindsight to place such importance on the denial of the daily transcript. But Perry, the court reporter, was getting sicker day by day and died before he had the opportunity to transcribe his shorthand notes. Likely the quality of his notes deteriorated with his health. Later, a dreadful mess resulted when a substitute, Stanley Fraser, attempted to read and transcribe the notes. Questions were raised about Fraser's transcription, and the fact that he was related to Prosecutor Leavy and was an alcoholic. Had there been a daily record, the fact that the court reporter died shortly after the completion of the trial would have been immaterial. The record already would have been available in reasonably complete form. Errors in transcription could have been caught and corrected within twenty-four hours. And if the record showed that Perry was failing in health the judge could have had him replaced. Thus, there would have been no need for a substitute transcriber after the trial.

As the trial drew to a close, Judge Fricke came forth with another unusual ruling. Of his own volition, he informed Chessman that either he or his legal advisor, Al Matthews, could sum up to the jury; but not both of them. The plan Chessman had worked out had been for Matthews to argue the technical points concerning kidnapping law and Chessman to argue on the factual points that indicated his innocence. When faced with choosing between them, Chessman, as expected, opted to handle the closing arguments himself rather than have Matthews do it.

As with other tricky rulings by Judge Fricke, the first question is, "Could he legally do it?" The answer, as always, is, probably yes. The second question is, "Why did he do it?" This is harder to answer. Within the broad powers of a trial judge is the capacity to regulate the number of attorneys who can address the court and jury during a trial. This power is given to a judge so as to prevent the badgering of both witnesses and jury and to cut down on confusion and prejudicial feelings. Each defendant, of course, may employ his own attorney. Other than this concession, courts often require that the attorney who starts to cross-examine a witness must handle all dealings with this witness. The purpose is to keep order and not submit a nervous, tiring witness to a whole barrage of freshly rested shock troops alternating in their attempts to break down his story.

There existed a California statute specifically permitting two attorneys for each side to address the jury on summation in capital cases. Technically speaking, Al Matthews was not an attorney in this case. He was, at Chessman's insistence, merely a legal advisor. So, one could say Chessman had only one attorney, himself. But if this were the proper interpretation, Fricke should have ordered Chessman to do all the arguing to the jury and never allowed Chessman to substitute Matthews. However, Judge Fricke had permitted Matthews to cross-examine Chessman when he took the stand on his own behalf and Matthews had questioned Hallie Chessman, Caryl's dying mother, when it would have been too much to expect that Chessman could calmly pose questions to his obviously suffering mother. Since Matthews had appeared in the case to this extent, what harm could it have done to permit him to handle the technical part of the argument to the jury? The answer, of course, is none!

Finally, there is the matter of Chessman's claim three or four years after the trial that, at one point during the deliberations, when the jurors came back for instructions, Fricke told them that "the defendant was one of the worst criminals he had had in his court and the jury should bring in the death penalty." If true, this would constitute an error necessitating reversal of the convictions. All but Chessman's extreme supporters believe that this tale is a fabrication of Chessman's imagination. But a lot of people who don't believe the story do not think that Fricke was unfair, only that he was too smart to give Chessman such a golden opportunity to get off the hook. The tale does not make sense to me because it is unlikely that, after thirty days of studious concentration upon observance of all the forms, Fricke would have thrown it all away in a careless emotional display at the end of the trial.

On the same basis, one can be dubious of a charge against Judge Fricke made by Machlin and Woodfield in *Ninth Life*. These reporters located a California lawyer who claimed that in the course of occasional conversations in the corridor during the trial Fricke had told him he was furious with Chessman's wise-guy tactics and promised he would take care of him. In addition, we should be skeptical of the story because the attorney asked to remain anonymous (on the grounds that judges of the California Supreme Court would take revenge against him on behalf of their besmirched colleague), and because he waited twelve years (during which time Fricke had died) to tell the story.

Even if Fricke ran a "fair trial" in the sense that the law was not broken, it is entirely another thing to say that Fricke ran a "fair trial" in the sense that every possible step was taken to conform to the fundamental American tenet that every man is innocent until proven guilty. No trial is fair if this does not happen. The reader can judge whether this happened in Chessman's case. Was Chessman treated by Judge Fricke as truly innocent until proven guilty? Or was the feeling of the judge, "I think you are guilty and we are going to observe every rule so that the jury will have the chance to find you guilty"?

Judge Fricke should not be made out to be uniquely brutal or vicious. He was simply an ordinary human being. He possessed a firm set of ideas and, like most people, found it difficult to submerge totally his personal feelings when dealing with someone who lived under a different type of personal code. American legal history has too many examples of extreme judicial prejudice. This is not what we are talking about with Judge Fricke. It was perfectly legitimate for him to abhor the crimes with which Chessman was charged and to be appalled by his disrespectful manner. But a judge must always insure that the defendant receives the fullest possible opportunity to contrast his version of the facts with that presented by the prosecution. Judge Fricke could have done much more in this regard. Although higher courts did not find judicial error in Fricke's handling of the case sufficient to mandate a new trial, Fricke's actions do not stand as a model of American justice.

In one sense, to criticize Judge Fricke is to criticize America in 1948. He was a highly representative specimen. America was passing through a period of moral absolutism, both righteous and frightened. These were the years of pride in American power which had triumphed in World War II, of frustration with postwar difficulties, and fear of nuclear holocaust. Also frightening to some in those years was the rapidity with which American life seemed to be changing and they responded by trying to freeze norms of conduct, whether for political power, dissent, race relations, or sexual activities. Regardless of whether Chessman did or did not commit the crimes with which he was charged, one can guess that to many Americans he seemed to typify all that was wrong in America, the way moral values were being trampled on by the young. In a word, he had no respect. It does not seem unreasonable to see Judge Fricke as a representative of this part of America.

Thus, Fricke approached the Chessman case with what one might call legal moral absolutism. By this is meant a judicial attitude which includes the belief that morality is falling apart and the conviction that the law must be used rigorously to restore the old standards. When an aggressively moral attitude is transferred to the practical sphere of a criminal case, the danger lurks that the defendant will be prosecuted as much for his unsatisfactory attitudes as for his crimes. This is especially true when the crimes are of a sexual nature. The kind of thinking involved in legal moral absolutism is reflected in the following statement by Eugene Williams, longtime Los Angeles attorney and prosecutor. It is quoted from J. Paul De River's *The Sexual Criminal: A Psychoanalytic Study*, published in 1956, in the belief

that it can give us an insight into the era of the Chessman trial
and the attitudes of Judge Fricke.

> In a world where living has become more complex; where nerves
> are keyed to a higher pitch; where spiritual values have been
> entirely forgotten; where religion has been displaced by a pseudo-
> intellectual and pseudo-scientific conglomeration of half baked
> superficialities which individuals are pleased to call their
> "philosophies of life;" in a world where there are no ethics except
> that of "not getting caught;" where there is no set principle of
> right and wrong; where children are brought into the world and
> educated according to the principle that a child should be
> permitted to express its own personality without restriction; where
> discipline and self-restraint and consideration for the rights of
> others are neglected as old fashioned and too difficult; in a world
> where the philosophy that "I will try anything once" is considered
> a satisfactory attitude for the young and inquiring mind; in a
> world where there is too little religion and too much idle time;
> there has developed a startling and dangerous increase in sex
> perversion.
>
> . . . I have come to the firm belief that the sex pervert is an
> individual of whom society should take note. I am sure that he is
> seldom insane in any sense which would lawfully permit him to be
> incarcerated in an insane asylum. I am sure that he is just as much
> a criminal as is the burglar or murder. I am also convinced that
> penitentiaries such as we have now, provide no place for his
> punishment or rehabilitation. In short, I believe that the sex
> pervert should be treated not as a patient but as a criminal. To
> punish him, however, he should be placed in an institution where
> the proper kind of rehabilitory work can be done so that, if
> capable of being brought to a realization of the errors of his ways,
> he may be brought back to society prepared to live as a normal,
> law abiding individual, rather than turned out as he now is from
> the penitentiary, confirmed in his perversion.

If Judge Fricke did not protect the rights of Chessman in an
adequate manner, his failure must be shared by the citizens, the
newspapers and all of the courts of 1948. Fricke, in the main,
conformed to 1948 standards of a fair trial, although certainly not
to the standards of a model trial. If one can say that a trial by

1948 standards was not a fair trial, then blame must be placed on American society in general and not just its representative in the courtroom. The actions of Judge Fricke are an accurate mirror of American societal attitudes in that period of our history. Chessman was the wrong type of personality, living in the wrong age, and charged with the kind of crimes the 1948 public could not accept.

7

Police Procedures: The Identifications

Now that conduct of the prosecutor and trial judge have been examined for bias, the next important area to examine is the identification of Chessman by witnesses. Earlier in this book, attention was given to the possibility of visual error in the identification of Chessman by witnesses. But Chessman claimed that the police used improper procedures in getting the identifications. The disputed identifications became important when Judge Fricke permitted them to be placed in evidence. Courts can do little to eliminate errors in identification caused by mistaken human judgement; but the courts can and must make sure that police do not unduly influence the process. Specifically, did the police procedures used in the identifications of Caryl Chessman satisfy constitutional standards of fairness? If not, because of the important role of the identifications in the case, Chessman did not receive a fair trial.

As discussed earlier, establishing guilt by eyewitness identification is inherently risky. Frequently the witness, especially if it is the victim, is too agitated to be careful in his observations, and even under the best of circumstances, memory is often unreliable. Moreover it can play tricks. Once a witness has identified someone as the culprit, any second attempt must override the visual picture already imprinted on the mind of the witness from the first identification. Most likely he will identify the same man the second time. There is no way of knowing whether his memory has reverted to the date of the crime, or only back to the first identification. Even the witness may never really know. Add to this the human desire not to be proven wrong, and it becomes clear that the crucial point is when the first identification is made. Lastly, despite their doubtful accuracy, eyewitness identifications have a powerful effect upon a jury, and are usually accepted no matter how much contrary evidence exists. The Chessman case is a perfect example: The defendant virtually stood on his head to draw the jury's attention away from the identifications, but he was unsuccessful.

Given these inherent problems, the methods police use to obtain identifications become all the more important. If an honest witness were beaten, bribed or threatened by the police to identify a particular suspect as the criminal in question, he would refuse to knuckle under. But the police can give the witness a "nudge" in the right direction. By various methods, some extremely subtle and ingenious, it is possible for the police to add elements to the subconscious of the witness that will influence his judgment. Even after the witness is home in his easy chair, he will still think the identification procedure was on the level and that his superior eyesight and memory saved the day. The reader may wonder how in fact the police can plant the idea that the witness should choose a specific person out of a line-up. Here is an illustration. Suppose that I am held up while walking along Main Street. I tell the police that the robber was a six-foot four-inch black man, weighing around 220 pounds, wearing a green windbreaker, dungarees and a hat, and who spoke with a lisp. Three days later, the police call and ask me to come to the station to view the line-up. Already the strong possibility of the guilt of one of the men in the line-up has been planted in my mind. Why else would the police have me come down and view suspects if they were not reasonably sure that one was the man who had robbed me? This type of police influence is unavoidable. Courts permit this type of influencing witnesses as long as police don't call and say: "We have the man. Come down and pick him out." (That sort of statement is forbidden because it could eliminate in the minds of the witnesses the real possibility that none of the line-up participants is the guilty party.)

In the hypothetical example, seven different line-ups are presented to me. In the first, all participants are five-feet eight-inches tall except for one man six-feet four-inches tall. In the second, all are Caucasians except for one black man. In the third, all weigh under 150 pounds except for one 220-pound heavy-weight. In the four ensuing line-ups, all men but one wear topcoats, wear suit pants, are bare headed, and speak in a normal manner, while there is only one man in a green windbreaker, in dungarees, in a hat, and one man with a lisp. The odd man out in each of the seven separate line-ups is the same man.

This description is a parody; but the point is serious. It is not necessary for a policeman to get up close to the witness and whisper in his ear, "The guy on the end did it." There are many more devious ways to plant the idea, and once planted, it will stay there. Courts are justified in demanding that the first time the identification process is carried out, proper procedure is observed or the whole thing is null and void, and guilt must be proven without the aid of the improper identification. This is called, poetically, "the poisoned fruit" doctrine. In the same manner that one bad piece of fruit can infect a whole basket of it, one bad identification can spoil all subsequent identifications by the same witness. If the initial identification is not discovered to have been improper until after it has been admitted as evidence in a trial, it may be necessary to throw out the decision in the case and start over.

The police have not been portrayed in the best light in this identification discussion, but abuses are rare. However, it should be recognized that the police are not disinterested seekers of the truth. This is partly a matter of human nature. They are exposed to crime all day long. They risk their lives to apprehend criminals. They have seen too many truly guilty criminals declared innocent because of errors in proof, arbitrary jury decisions or changes of story by witnesses. On the whole, police do not arrest men that they do not think guilty. This brings forth a natural tendency to firm up their case as much as possible in order to diminish the possibility that other exigencies will intervene to frustrate the orderly workings of justice. It is frightening what aberrations from orderly norms of human conduct one will permit himself because he is convinced that his cause is good. One cannot condemn improper police pressure during investigation too strongly. It has no place in a democracy.

Recently, particularly in the years when Earl Warren was Chief Justice, the Supreme Court has been increasingly rigorous in defining constitutional requirements of fairness in police procedures. Beginning with a decision in 1957 that barred confessions secured by extended grilling before arraignment, a series of decisions (including the Escobedo and Miranda cases) significantly expanded the rights of defendants and put restraints on police actions. For our purposes it is important that in the 1960s judicial decisions tightened requirements for police procedures in identification of criminal suspects, in particular by insuring a suspect legal counsel from the moment of arrest, including at a line-up. The tightening occurred because courts became convinced that there were occasions when the police rigged identifications so as to induce the witness to identify one particular suspect. There are signs that the court led by Justices selected by Nixon may be backing away from some of the limitations on police actions, but clearly had Chessman's case been tried now or even in 1968 instead of 1948 the story of his trial would be different. Police procedures today are different from those of 1948. Three major identifications in the Chessman case will be examined by the standards of 1948 and those of today.

The first Chessman identification was that made by Mary Alice Meza from her second-story window. In legal parlance, this is called a "one-to-one identification." As the name connotes, the witness is brought face to face with the accused and asked if the accused is the one who committed the crime. No line-up occurs and no other suspects are presented. This was a frequently-used type of identification procedure in those days. Today it is outlawed except for one restricted exception: "on the spot identifications." These occur when the police apprehend a suspect within a short time of the commission of the crime. Since the trail is still warm, courts hold it permissible to confront the witness with the suspect. Police need to know right away if they have the right man. If not, they can resume the hunt before time and distance obscure the trail of the real assailant. Speed is considered so necessary that the consequent infringement of the rights of a defendant is considered relatively less important than the time that would be wasted waiting for the appearance of his attorney. Until very recently, courts have strictly limited the use of this kind of identification. The recent United States Supreme Court decision in *Kirby* v. *Illinois* shows a regrettable weakening of this concept.

Despite *Kirby*, the present-day "on the spot identification" exception could not be applied to the procedure by which Chessman was identified by Mary Alice Meza. The Meza identification occurred fifteen hours after the arrest of Chessman, and eighty-two hours after the attack. Clearly, the present-day "on the spot identification" technique could not be used in such a case. That being so, there would be no possibility, today, that Mary Alice could lean out her window and through swollen eyes, finger the still-handcuffed Chessman. Nowadays, because "one-to-one identifications" are pretty much a thing of the past, a sexually abused young girl like Miss Meza would have to come to the police station for identification purposes. If she were too ill to leave her room and still too emotionally distraught, the identification would have to wait. By the time she was able to come, her physical and emotional states presumably would be improved. And she would be obliged to pick her attacker from a whole group of suspects.

But even if present-day law did not apply in 1948, there was no excuse for seeking an identification from a girl whose face was swollen to twice its normal size and whose eyes were swollen practically shut. Add to this her mentally agitated state and the fact that she was at a distance of fifty feet from the man she identified and fifteen feet above him, one has to question whether it is at all possible to believe in the accuracy of her accusation. Her condition left her susceptible to identifying the first suspect with the slightest resemblance to her attacker, and it was most unlikely that she would ever go back on that first identification. The police deserve strong condemnation for procuring an identification under such improper circumstances.

Even by 1948 standards, it is questionable that the Meza identification should have been permitted into courtroom evidence. More importantly, it never should have taken place. Police seemed to have used it as a bargaining counter to get Chessman to confess to a whole string of crimes. They must have known that the girl was in no condition to make a reliable identification. It seems reasonable to think that they thought a quick identification by Meza, no matter how unreliable, would put Chessman in a bargaining mood. The police statement that after the Meza identification Chessman confessed (which, however, Chessman denied) suggests that the idea is not without foundation. When one comes right down to it, the effect was the same as if the police had beaten Chessman. Although Chessman would never have listened to an attorney, no competent attorney would have permitted his client to try and bargain with authorities as a result of an identification by such an obviously ill girl.

Because she was young, appealing, and pathetic, the identification by Miss Meza was of maximum courtroom importance. There is no way of knowing how much of an influence the identification had on Chessman's convictions on other charges in the case. Jury outrage caused by the Meza identification could have led to suppression of what would otherwise seem to be "reasonable doubt" as to the guilt of Chessman in some of the other crimes. Nothing herein should be construed to mean that Mary Alice was objectively wrong when she identified Chessman. However, the author believes that although she positively identified Chessman, there was no way that she could have been positive. The fault is less hers than that of the police who took advantage of her condition in order to slam the door shut on Chessman, and the judge who allowed the identification in evidence. Its inflamatory content, when repeated to a jury, must have gravely hurt Chessman's cause. In any event, we are a long way from exemplary justice.

The Meza identification was not the only unusual one

occurring in the case. The first identification meeting between Mrs. Johnson and Chessman was also out of the ordinary. Police had telephoned to ask her and Lea to come to the police station in order to view a line-up. While walking down a corridor toward the line-up room, Mr. and Mrs. Johnson and Mr. Lea passed an open door. Guess who just happened to be sitting in the room? Lea pointed out Chessman to Mrs. Johnson. They agreed that he was the "red light bandit." (It should be recalled that Lea never saw Chessman without a mask on the night of the crime.) It is hard to believe that this confrontation was accidental. It planted a recent picture of Chessman in the consciousness of the two witnesses, and the odds were increased that they would pick him out of the line-up and identify him as the "red light bandit." At any rate, Lea and Mrs. Johnson arrived at the line-up already convinced that Chessman was the "red light bandit."

Accidental confrontations are sometimes still permitted today. In a recent case the judge allowed in evidence an identification in which the witness who identified the suspect had sat unobtrusively in the corner of a police station, observing everyone who walked through the door during a period of an hour. This type of accidental encounter is preferable to the one used in the Chessman case because that was a one-to-one encounter, eliminating the necessity of choosing from a large group, and strongly suggesting the guilt of one man. Because "one-to-one" identifications were entirely permissible in 1948, the procedure can only be disapproved and not condemned, even though a man's life was at stake. Similarly, it is unfortunate that Mrs. Johnson did not first see Chessman when she was alone and not subject to immediate corroboration by Lea; there is a natural tendency to agree with a friend. Thus, while the procedures in this identification were not as outrageous as in the Meza identification, they were inappropriate in 1948 and would probably be illegal today.

The third identification was made by a number of witnesses who viewed a large line-up, conducted in the usual fashion. Even this procedure ended up as a source of dispute and controversy. A total of fifty men were placed on the lighted stage. Chessman, Knowles and four others were selected by the witnesses as possible participants in the various crimes committed against them. The crimes in question included more than the "red light crimes," and as a result the housebreaking and Pasadena clothing-store offenses were added to the charges against Chessman. One witness asked to see the six men while wearing handkerchief masks. Given the *modus operandi* of the "red light bandit," this was a reasonable request. A policeman reached up to tie a handkerchief around the face of Chessman. He grabbed for the handkerchief, tied it himself and, according to the husband of Regina Johnson, said "Don't bother. I know how I wore it." If true, this would be a very damaging admission. But Chessman claimed he said: "Don't bother. I know how I wear it." This would turn the statement from an admission of guilt into a statement concerning his trade, being a professional thief. Chessman was the first to say that he was a professional thief, so admitting that he had a normal manner of wearing a handkerchief mask would say nothing definite about this particular case.

Chessman attacked this line-up on the grounds that the police called all the witnesses and said: "We have captured the 'red light bandit.' Come down and identify him!" As noted earlier, this would be improper, if true. Both police and witnesses denied it. Common sense requires us to accept the unanimous denial, especially because Chessman could not have known what the police said on the phone to the witnesses. More serious is his claim that police asked him a disproportionate amount of questions during the line-up. The purpose of questions at such a time is supposed to be only for voice identification. However, a cagey police sergeant can use the questions to focus the attention of witnesses on one suspect which might lead them to identify him. This trick is still used to some extent today, but the fact that a suspect can be represented at the line-up by an attorney of his choice tends to discourage its employment. The police did not deny that they questioned Chessman more than the others. The reason, they said, was that he gave provocative answers. This really is no justification, but it is the sort of error that courts rarely correct. If this identification line-up had occurred today, it probably would have run much the same way as it did a quarter of a century ago, particularly since one can guess that even today and even in a line-up Chessman would insist on being his own lawyer.

There is considerable ground for doubt about the accuracy of some of the identifications. In part, this is because of the discrepancies between the original descriptions of the bandit's height and weight and Chessman's physique, and also because of the emotional state of some of the major witnesses. In addition, the police used some unusual methods to get them. But on the whole, the methods employed for obtaining the identifications at the police station were tolerable, if not good. Even today, the line-up would come close to passing inspection, and so would the accidental spotting of Chessman by Mrs. Johnson and Lea because they had a chance to see other possible suspects in the line-up. But despite the various reasons for doubt about the identifications, in his instructions to the jury Judge Fricke did not stress that there might be any question about them. And the jurors seem to have accepted the major identifications without question, rejecting only that given by Mary Tarro when they found Chessman innocent of the housebreaking charge.

The only one of the three identifications that would not pass today is the Meza identification. It was a shocking denial of Chessman's constitutional rights, both by the standards of that day and of the present. The results of this identification should never have been admitted into evidence. Moreover, it is highly questionable whether, once admitted into evidence, this was not a serious enough error to necessitate a reversal of all seventeen subsequent convictions. Judges are human and errors occur. But an error of this magnitude is not permissible. But when all is taken together, it seems to me that while the identification part of the Chessman case was by no means perfect, justice was not perverted except in the horror show surrounding the Meza identification. Police procedures used in the identifications are not sufficient cause to say that Chessman did not have a fair trial.

8

Chessman's Confession

The police story is that shortly after Mary Alice Meza identified him from her second-story window, Chessman admitted that he had committed many of the crimes with which he was charged. The policemen who interrogated Chessman testified at the trial that he had admitted robbing the dentist, Bartle, and the truck salesman, Stone, and had said that he drove Mary Alice Meza around for a couple of hours but then had a change of heart about raping her because she seemed very young. The police also maintained that earlier in the interrogation, Chessman had admitted the Redondo Beach robbery while, at the same time, irrationally trying to protect David Knowles by claiming that he had committed the crime without any help from Knowles or anyone else. Chessman did not deny the police claim that he had confessed. But his version is significantly different:

> At the trial two irreconcilably conflicting versions were given of what was said and what transpired while I was held at the station. I testified that I was beaten brutally, denied sleep, threatened with further violence, not allowed to see an attorney or my father, grilled to exhaustion and promised only two or three robbery charges would be filed if I confessed to the "red light" crimes;

that the police threatened to send me to the gas chamber if I refused to confess, or kill me if I failed to do so and then claim that I had been attempting to escape; and that as a result, when these physical and psychological third-degree methods became intolerable, I falsely and involuntarily agreed to anything that the police said when the words were put into my mouth.

Was Chessman brutally beaten? In those days, the law allowed the police seventy-two hours of interrogation before they had to charge a man or allow him legal counsel. Abuses often occured. Today, by Supreme Court decision, a man has a right to a lawyer from the moment that serious interrogation begins and can refuse to answer any questions except in the presence of his attorney. But Chessman lacked this protection. During the seventy-two hour interrogation period he lost twelve pounds. This could be indicative of improper treatment, although it could just as easily be the result of poor prison food and anxiety. There was also direct testimony at the trial that Chessman had been beaten. Harold Gibson, a fellow prisoner with Chessman, recounted:

The first thing that came to my attention was your face. One of your cheek bones was swollen and discolored. There was also a gash at the hairline. I believe on the left hand side. In addition to that, one thumb was dislocated or fractured, was bent over the back of the hand. It was somewhat swollen. Then you showed me both shins were bloody and raw from your knees to your ankles....Your chest was black and blue as far as I could see... your entire chest was discolored.

One might think that a wise guy like Chessman would be a natural target for any aggressive policemen. He was a well-known bad character, strongly suspected of sex crimes. For this reason, many people believed Chessman when he said he was beaten. Once this contention is accepted, it is an easy next step to dismiss his confessions. My view is that Chessman was not beaten in the sense of being physically abused by police officers. In part, this is because of what earlier has been called Chessman's "overactive imagination." Secondly, at the trial all of the police who testified, and the prison doctor and male nurse who supervised the prison hospital, insisted that Chessman had not been beaten. It seems unlikely that there would be such unanimity if such testimony constituted perjury.

Lastly, one can cite Chessman's personality. The police would not have beaten Chessman because there would have been no need to do so. Given his ego, a little flattery would have caused him to fall over backwards to impress police with his criminal prowess. Consider the following examples from Chessman's trial testimony. The first quote deals with Chessman's recollection concerning part of the subject matter of the interrogation and shows his pride that the police were aware of his exploits:

> They started kidding me about this time up in the Flintridge Hills where two men and myself took guns and a squad car away from two deputies up there. They started talking about some gun play we had had with the State Highway Patrol in 1941. They were remembering those things.

Imagine the effect this must have had on a jury! The second statement by Chessman was meant to show his innocence by pointing to the fact that he did not try hard to escape arrest by Officers Riordan and May:

> It was not because I lost my guts . . . I have been in cases before where officers have shot at me. I have testified that my partners actually have been shot down beside me. I didn't lose my guts then . . . and I do think that I should show you that regardless of my past record, if I did have a knowledge of these crimes I would not have dropped my gun and run.

Chessman's claim that all but two or three robbery charges would be ignored if he confessed to the "red light" crimes does not ring true. Police don't make deals unless they have something to gain. In this instance, nothing seems to offer itself as a reason for a deal. Chessman had no knowledge as to crimes other than his own. Police felt that they had enough to convict Chessman without a confession. A guilty plea would not so lessen the expense to the state for trying him that it would be worth making a deal. None of the traditional reasons that motivate police to obtain prosecution agreement for a deal are present. Besides, the seriousness of the charges, the sexual outrage, Chessman's lack of cooperation with authorities, belligerent attitude and recidivism all strongly suggest that the police would not have offered a deal even if they had something to gain by it. It is hard to believe Chessman's account that he was beaten brutally for not accepting a deal, when common sense dictates that no deal ever was offered for him to refuse.

Despite this, there was a loophole which allowed doubt to persist about the confession story. First of all, Chessman's confession was not in writing. That is not too surprising, because Chessman was much too cagey a customer to have signed a confession. But, during the trial and after, Chessman always asked to take a lie detector test with the policemen who allegedly beat him into confession, and the State of California refused to give him that test or to order the policemen in question to prove their story by taking such a test. Thus, the next problem is why there was not a lie detector test. The answers here must be speculative, but it seems likely that the prosecutors clearly felt they had enough evidence to convict Chessman without a lie detector test. Besides, the test is not sufficiently reliable to be admissible in court. After the trial, the authorities probably wanted to avoid giving Chessman a test because they could be pretty sure that he could use the test, no matter what the results, as the basis for a long set of appeals.

However, it is incontestable that the jury gave great weight to the testimony that Chessman had confessed to some of the crimes with which he was charged. The State of California should have taken more precautions in this case, a capital one, to lay to rest every doubt as to whether Chessman's constitutional rights had indeed been violated, as he alleged. And it would have been most appropriate for the governor to take the results of a lie detector test into account in his decision on whether to commute Chessman's death sentence. Such a decision is a matter of discretion and a governor is free to employ any reasonable criteria, even those not admissible as evidence in court. Thus, it was clearly a mistake to refuse Chessman a lie detector test. The reason for the refusal, in my view, was not the fear that Chessman would be proven to be telling the truth, but rather because of his arrogant and irritating personality. If he had said he did *not* want to take a lie detector test, probably nine policemen would have immediately strapped him down to take one. Chessman had the knack of making otherwise rational people act irrationally, or at the least, highly imprudently.

More difficult to understand is why the defense did not try harder to obtain a lie detector test for Chessman. It cannot have been a matter of the cost. Although Chessman may have been indigent at the time of his trial, he certainly was not later on, during the years of appeals. The profits from *Cell 2455, Death Row* alone, to say nothing of his other books, must have been considerable. In addition, he received financial contributions from individuals and groups opposed to capital punishment. Even the problem of obtaining permission from prison authorities would not have been insurmountable. If the authorities refused, it seems certain that in the early 1950s the court would have overruled them, as was done in a whole group of related demands by Chessman. Despite initial refusal by prison officials, Chessman eventually received permission from the courts to obtain a cell for preparing appeals, to acquire a typewriter and law books, and to have unobstructed access to his attorney in a conference room. After February 1, 1955, the court withdrew these rights, but permission to take a lie detector test might have been treated differently.

The conclusion, then, is that the defense attorneys did not believe that such a test would help Chessman. A good defense attorney does not necessarily have to believe the story of his client, especially if his client is an habitual criminal. While we do not know what Chessman told his attorneys, we do know that he often lied on other occasions. It seems probable the attorneys thought that a lie detector test would cook Chessman's goose for good, and that it was a prudent move on their part not to insist on one. Moreover, it seems likely that if Chessman had flunked the test he would have launched a whole barrage of new appeals, claiming that the machine was improperly balanced and falsely certified by the Department of Weights and Measures, or that the technician running the machine had looked cross-eyed at him. And his attorneys would have known that more objections and appeals would only have further alienated an already totally unsympathetic judiciary.

If, as is here argued, Chessman did confess to police officers, it is necessary to suggest an explanation for his motivation. As a parolee, he knew that a new conviction would necessitate serving more of the unexpired term to which he had previously been sentenced. Therefore, any confession would have repercussions beyond simply serving time for the charges to which he pleaded guilty. Assuming he confessed without physical coercion, a sufficiently serious reason must have existed for doing so. This reason could be none other than the threat of the death penalty. Chessman must have known that transporting a person with intent to commit bodily harm (Sec. 209 kidnapping), as well as murder, espionage, trainwrecking, and prison violence by a lifer rated "the big one." The first time there was talk of a Sec. 209 charge, Chessman would have been less than an apathetic listener. In this context, the way the police arranged the hurried trip to see Mary Alice Meza becomes no random happening.

It must have left Chessman good and scared. Under such circumstances, it would stand to reason that Chessman would try, perhaps hesitantly, to work out a deal. A tribute to his fortitude, however misplaced it might be, is that he did not sing like a bird. An ordinary man would have come clean, in an instant.

Even though one can be pretty sure that Chessman was not beaten, the unorthodox confrontation with Mary Alice Meza had the same effect. One can almost imagine the dialogue. The policemen return Chessman to the squad car and, with a grin, someone says: "It's you, Caryl! She says it's you. Could be the big one. Better to come clean. No promises, understand. However, if you cooperate, we might be able to do something." The result is virtually preordained, as is the later refusal of the prosecutor to make a deal and Chessman's subsequent renunciation of the confession. No one would waste the time to try and make him sign anything. Both he and they would understand tacitly that after he confessed the next step would depend on whether the prosecutor was inclined to compromise.

The authorities definitely were sitting in the cat-bird seat. Both Mary Alice Meza and the Redondo Beach robbery were as close to sure things as any case could be before trial time. If they did not have Chessman for the gas chamber, they certainly did for a long jail term. His parole status would have been no secret to them. They could bargain hard. If Chessman tried to approach a deal in a theoretical, hypothetical manner, every policeman within five miles would yawn and say: "No fairy tales, Chessman. Give us some facts and then we will see. What did you do?" If he does give them the facts they can be used against him in court, and it has cost the police absolutely nothing. All they promised to do was listen.

Even though there could be no second-story identification today and no seventy-two hour interrogation period before bringing charges, if today Chessman refused to hire an attorney it is likely that his fate would be the same. An attorney could have bargained for Chessman as an intermediary. Since the attorney would have no fear of going to jail, the identification by Mary Alice Meza would not have produced the state of panic in him that it must have in Chessman. As an intermediary, an attorney bargaining over a possible deal for Chessman could discuss the facts in a manner impossible for Chessman. Not being dependent upon police favor, the way that his client would be, an attorney would have a lot more chance of making a deal for Chessman than he would for himself.

All in all, Chessman's story that his confessions were coerced by beatings do not ring true. One cannot visualize this tough professional confessing against his will unless he received the most fearful of beatings. The doctor and male nurse certainly would have recognized such a beating. The police had nothing to gain by a beating. The trial proved beyond a reasonable doubt that the quickest way to Chessman's heart was by flattery. His tales of other crimes that he had committed without detection and his wild driving exploits that allowed him to avoid capture, all were told as a result of prosecution flattery. He must have known the damage that these accounts would do to his case. Literally, he could not help himself. One must believe the same of the confession the police claim he made. Prudence would have dictated a discreet silence in the face of persistent police questioning, but when was Chessman ever prudent?

As a final point, it should be noted here that during the trial Chessman never advanced his theory that he was being framed by the mob. If this had really been true and he had been taken for a death ride in the desert as he later claimed, it would stand to reason that he would tell this to the police. Chessman's failure to broach this desert ride subject at all rather conclusively demonstrates that it was a later fabrication.

When making an overall judgment on the confession of Chessman, one comes to the same conclusion reached when examining the trial conduct of Prosecutor Leavy and Judge Fricke, and the identification methods employed by the Los Angeles Police Department. One would not want to use them as textbook examples. At the same time, it is impossible to state honestly that fundamental fairness was violated to a point that it would be necessary to reverse the convictions and give Chessman a new trial. One large exception to this basically favorable judgment must be emphasized. It does not include the disturbing incident at the home of Mary Alice Meza.

9

Beyond a
Reasonable Doubt?

Although it seems reasonable to conclude that Chessman received a fair trial in terms of the methods of the prosecutor, judge, and police, it is still necessary to ask whether the State of California proved its case against Chessman beyond a reasonable doubt. The jury found Chessman innocent of one charge against him, but on the other seventeen, all twelve jurors decided beyond a reasonable doubt that Chessman was guilty as charged. The question we must now turn to is one that bears on this question of reasonable doubt: Did the jury decide correctly? Was information withheld by the prosecution that might have affected their decision?

"Reasonable doubt" is a concept that has successfully escaped definition for centuries. There is an ephemeral quality to "reasonable doubt," because one is concerned with the mind and heart of another human being, the individual juror. The juror possesses a most burdensome power. As the community representative he must decide in the name of the community if enough evidence of guilt is present that the individual member of the community charged with a transgression ought to be judged culpable and consequently punished. He decides whether another human being is freed or is dispatched to the living hell of a prison or occasionally to death. No theoretician can provide the juror with a mathematical equation for deciding when there is no reasonable doubt of guilt. General guidelines can be advanced; more than that, nothing can be done but to trust the conscience of each individual juror.

Appellate courts are notoriously reluctant to overturn jury findings. Unless convinced that, upon the factual situation as developed at the trial, no correctly reasoning jury could possibly have found the defendant guilty beyond a reasonable doubt, the appellate court will permit the decision to stand. Of course, if the constitutional rights of the defendant were seriously violated by the admission of a coerced confession or improper actions of the judge or prosecutor, or in some other major matter, the conviction will have to be overturned. If this is done, the reason will be that the constitutional right of the defendant to a fair trial has been compromised, not that the jury unquestionably erred in finding the defendant guilty beyond a reasonable doubt. The appellate court, then, is not a second, supervening jury. Its function is not to second guess, but to act as the last resort if a clear miscarriage of justice has occurred.

Let us then turn to the jury and its verdicts. Chessman's jury included eleven women, most of them housewives and mothers of grown children. This fact is significant for several reasons. It is generally thought that women are more hesitant to vote for a guilty verdict, especially where the death penalty is involved, than are men. Given their votes to convict, one must think that the women jurors were fully satisfied that Chessman was guilty beyond a reasonable doubt. Secondly, attitudes of and toward women were different in 1948 (reflected in the fact that in those prewomen's lib days Judge Fricke unhesitatingly appointed the one male member of the jury as foreman) and it is probable that these women adhered to the more rigorous attitudes in sexual matters that were typical of 1948. This is related to the point made earlier that the Chessman case must be evaluated in the context of the values of 1948, not those of a quarter of a century later. One cannot be sure what effect the composition of the jury had on the Chessman trial, concerned as it was largely with sexual offenses, but it seems reasonable to think that it had some influence on the outcome.

In finding Chessman guilty on seventeen of the eighteen counts, the jury had to make 216 different decisions and of these 204 (94 percent) were that Chessman was guilty. That is, twelve average citizens rejected Chessman's alibis—that he was with friends or with his sick mother—in most all of the cases. Prosecutor Leavy's questioning left the various alibis in shattered pieces and neither Chessman's sworn testimony nor that of his mother or friends convinced the jury. We have already mentioned the jury's apparent lack of questions about the identifications.

The jury's verdicts also show that in addition to his alibis another of Chessman's lines of defense was rejected. He said that a professional criminal would not commit sex crimes and, moreover, would not bother with penny ante robberies. Apparently the jury thought professional criminals *could* sink to sex crimes and penny ante robberies, or else that Chessman was not really a professional criminal. The boldness of the professional criminal argument backfired on Chessman and probably served to resolve many doubts in the minds of the jurors. All jurors, at least implicitly, ask themselves if the defendant could indeed commit crimes. Is he that type of person? Chessman not only testified repeatedly that he was the type of person who could commit crime, but seemingly was proud of the fact that he often did so. Few jurors would make the neat distinction between sex crimes and other crimes the way Chessman did. The strategy was foolhardy. It alienated the jury. Just as importantly, it made it hard for any appellate court to reverse the conviction on the grounds that no jury could have convicted this man beyond a reasonable doubt. With Chessman eagerly seeking recognition as a member of the who's who of organized crime, how could any appellate court say that the jury's decision could not be justified under any circumstances? This does not mean that the jury decision was correct. It does mean that an appellate court was virtually powerless to overturn the conviction on "reasonable doubt" grounds.

While we can be sure that the jurors had resolved any reasonable doubt they might have about Chessman's guilt on the basis of the evidence presented, would their verdicts have been changed had more evidence or different evidence been presented? Chessman during the trial attacked the lack of scientific examination of the physical evidence to support the charges against him, in particular those alleging sexual attacks. Later he cited eight different instances where the prosecution failed to present scientific evidence:

1. No attempt was made to test Chessman's clothes for the presence of semen or the presence of hair from a woman's head.

2. The clothes of Mary Alice Meza never were checked for the presence of semen.

3. The clothes of Chessman were never shown to the witnesses for possible identification.

4. No semen sample was taken from Chessman for categorization and possible elimination. Such a test cannot prove positively that it was the semen of the suspect. Negatively, it can establish that it was not the semen of the defendant. This is the same principle as a blood test in a paternity suit. It is possible a sample of semen would have been found in the car or on the effects of one of the participants that could have been compared with the sample provided by Chessman.

5. The pistol that was thrown from the Ford at the time of the capture of Chessman was not laboratorily tested to see if it contained blood or skin of the owner of the Redondo Beach clothing store. This crime occurred within ninety minutes of the arrest—"hot evidence" in the truest sense of the term.

6. The Ford was not searched for any signs of blood, semen, or pubic hair. The seatcovers were never analyzed. This is most surprising because the prosecution maintained that the Ford in which Chessman was captured was the car in which he committed all, or virtually all, of the charged crimes.

7. The coat of Regina Johnson was never taken to a laboratory for investigation even though Lea had maintained from the time of his very first account to police that he had seen semen on her coat when she returned to his car.

8. The spotlight of the Ford was never examined scientifically

for traces of a red piece of cellophane. The police came up with this theory because the spotlight was white, not red. It was necessary to give a satisfactory explanation for the unanimous opinion of all witnesses that the spotlight was red, not white.

The prosecution conducted their case as if the laboratory part of their operation was taking a month's holiday. Scientific evidence was most sketchy and ill-prepared; even when the appropriate tests were made, they generally were done so long after the events as to render all findings inconclusive. This is not a case in which the prosecution made the tests, then did not like the results and sat on them. It simply is a case where no one got around to making them. Prosecutor Leavy summed it up when he observed during the argument to the jury that "we can't think of everything."

Scientific tests are not an obligatory part of a prosecution. In this case, authorities had ample evidence without resorting to scientific tests. It is quite possible that the results would have been inconclusive, anyway. If so, little would have been lost. The prosecution would not have had any obligation to present the results in court. On the other hand, results might have been positive. This could have served to nail down any remaining serious doubt that a juror might have possessed that the attacks in question occurred. The omission of scientific tests could have had disastrous consequences to the prosecution's case. It didn't, but Leavy's statement, "We can't think of everything" is not a valid excuse. This is one thing that should have been thought of. This does not mean that the rights of Chessman were compromised by the failure to make these tests. It does mean that an opportunity to add even more logs to the fire proving the guilt of Chessman was ignored.

Then there is the charge made by Machlin and Woodfield that prosecution sources withheld the reports first given by Mrs. Johnson and Miss Meza on their initial interview by police. If these reports were truly different from later accounts by the two women, a reasonable doubt could occur in the minds of the jurors, at least as to the convictions for crimes concerning those two women. Machlin and Woodfield make much of the fact that no description of the actual act of oral intercourse appears in either preliminary report. Consistent with their obviously slanted approach in favor of Chessman, the authors take this as clear indication that such intercourse never occurred. If this is so, the bodily harm necessary for the conviction of a Sec. 209 kidnapping charge is absent, and without it there could have been no death sentence. If their conclusion is correct, the prosecution would be obliged to make this report available even if the defendant had not made a request to see it.

The ticklish issue of evidence withheld by the prosecution is a necessary by-product of our adversary system of justice. All prosecutors are charged with protecting the community by prosecuting those who transgress the laws of the community. However, since the defendant is a citizen, he is at the same time one of those whom the prosecutor is sworn to protect. Appellate courts, always quick to throw in theoretical guidelines that often read prettily but are hard to apply, have proposed a solution for prosecutors unsure whether they must show a piece of evidence to the defense. If the piece of evidence in question would tend either to change the case radically or give clear indication of the innocence of the defendant, its contents should be made available to the defendant. In 1972, the Supreme Court of California overturned a conviction in which the prosecution presented as a witness against the defendant a man who had thirty-seven convictions on his record. The court found an absolute obligation on the part of the prosecution to apprise the defendant of the criminal record of the witness. Failure to do so resulted in a reversal of a conviction that was otherwise valid.

It is unlikely that the first reports by Mrs. Johnson and Miss Meza fall into the category demanding obligatory prosecution disclosure. The emotional state of the women makes these reports of questionable reliability. The judicial guideline does not cover evidence that might favor the defendant, only that which incontestably does so. Any defense counsel would have wanted to see the first reports made by these women. He would naturally be suspicious when they were not forthcoming. A legal procedure known as "discovery" exists for obtaining documents held by the other side. Undoubtedly these disclosure possibilities were known to Chessman's legal advisor, Al Matthews. But as we know, advising Chessman would be a most difficult task. Nonetheless, it does seem that somehow or other, he should have convinced Chessman to demand the production, in court, of these initial reports. The demand, however, was not made.

Quite possibly Mrs. Johnson and Miss Meza did not furnish details of the act of oral intercourse in their first accounts to the police. It cannot be said that this in itself indicates that they later changed their stories. The details they furnished on what led up to the attacks, and their emotional condition afterwards, seem to make it clear that the attacks did, in fact, occur. Since this is so, the later and more complete accounts superceded these preliminary reports and the prosecution was not required to provide the preliminary reports to Chessman unless specifically requested to do so. Theoretically, justice is not totally served if the prosecutor can choose to present only his best evidence and hide the rest. However, questions of efficiency and order dictate permitting the prosecution to choose its best evidence. The defendant can resort to subpoena, cross-questioning, and discovery to supplement and expose what the prosecution does not choose to introduce into the case.

This discussion of the prosecution's obligation to share evidence with the defendant leads to a most fundamental point of our judicial system, one already referred to in the chapter on the prosecutor: Ours is an adversarial, not a cooperative, system. A criminal trial is not a disinterested search for "truth." The prosecution and the defense are not on equal footing. The people have the right to be protected from criminals. By the act of indicting the defendant, any bonds of friendship between the people and him are in abeyance until the resolution of the charges against him. To pretend in court that we are all pals in this together goes a long way toward defeating the purpose of a criminal trial. Pretty rules of courtroom decorum aside, a criminal trial is a knockdown, drag-out fight, seeking to deprive the defendant of the thing most precious to him except for his life: his liberty. It isn't pretty, and pretending it is doesn't make it so.

From this view of a trial, it flows logically that the prosecution is not required to continue to eliminate all conceivable doubt as to the guilt of the defendant once the verdict is in. Chessman and his supporters acted as if every new postconviction argument they dreamed up (and the number runs to hundreds) should bring all the wheels of justice to a grinding halt, obliging everyone to devote full time to establishing the truth about the latest brainstorm. That is not the proper function of the authorities. A man who has been found guilty in the adversarial judicial system is, for the purposes of the system, truly guilty. This does not mean that the door is definitively shut. If new evidence can be produced, it will be considered. In order to necessitate a new trial, this evidence must clearly and convincingly demonstrate the likelihood that the defendant would be found innocent at a new trial. The burden falls totally on the defendant.

In this context, Chessman's evasiveness about telling all he knew becomes ludicrous. His cryptic little sayings, his use of pseudonyms in his "true story" book accounts, and his contradicting sets of accounts of his actions during the forty-six days before his arrest, are far short of the clear and convincing evidence that a man who has been convicted must show to get a new trial. The ball was entirely with Chessman. He failed to carry it. Maybe Chessman was not the "red light bandit." But if he wasn't, I am confident he knew who was. The responsibility was all his, either to point the finger or take the consequences. This is an area in which the state authorities cannot be faulted. Chessman had only himself to blame.

A rather full summary has been made of the question of "reasonable doubt." Each reader can take into account the factual situation for each crime and decide whether he has a reasonable doubt as to Chessman's guilt in that instance and thus would have opposed that particular conviction. Even if the reader does conclude that a reasonable doubt of guilt exists he must still remember that he was not in the courtroom during the trial. The manner of witnesses, the general attitude of Chessman, the persuasiveness of Prosecutor Leavy all could operate in actuality to throw what, in isolation, seems to be a reasonable doubt back into the realm of sufficient certainty. We can never know if this would have happened to us if we had been sitting as jury members because we were not there. The jury was there and it did not find a reasonable doubt seventeen out of eighteen times. Their own certainty seems clear. When we try to put ourselves back in the year 1948, it becomes hard to assert categorically that they erred.

10

The Death Penalty

The time has arrived to look at "the big one"—the death penalty. Even with all the drama and excitement that percolated through the Chessman case, it never would have reached world-wide prominence if it had not involved the death penalty. Death is final. No change in the law, no sort of rehabilitation, no new evidence, nothing can change the *fait accompli* of death. If the worst that faced Chessman had been a long stay at San Quentin, protest would have been much more moderate than it was. The chance that Chessman's fortunes could take a turn for the better would have tended to sap the fury of his supporters. *Time* does not run cover stories of lifers. Albert Einstein, Eleanor Roosevelt, the Queen Mother of Belgium, Marlon Brando, Steve Allen, and Brigitte Bardot do not get involved publicly in lesser cases. It was because of the possibility of capital punishment that the case received world-wide notice.

Over the course of the twelve-plus years encompassed by the Chessman case, the focus of controversy changed radically. At first, interest was centered on the question of the true guilt of Chessman and the fairness of his trial. As the temporal immediacy of these questions faded, the capital punishment aspect ascended to prominence. At the time of the trial, the ideological opponents of capital punishment were unaware of his case. It was only as the time he spent on Death Row began to lengthen that he drew attention. His best-selling autobiography made the real difference. Many of his new found anticapital punishment friends employed him simply as a vehicle in their attempt to abolish all capital punishment. Because his name was known, they threw their support to him. His innocence, or the question of whether he had received a fair trial, was of little interest to them. If he were truly innocent, or actually had not received a fair trial, so much the better. However, this all was peripheral to their belief that under no circumstances should the state be given the power to execute any citizen. The main thrust of the protest was taken out of the hands of Chessman and assumed by his special interest group of supporters.

It cannot be said that Chessman was unwilling to have his case become the focus of a campaign against capital punishment. Clearly, it was a subject in which he had more than a passing interest. In addition, Chessman loved attention of any type. He did not seem to mind being portrayed as a martyr. He took the role to heart and reveled in it. But near the end, when it was clear that execution could not be put off much longer, he seemed to think his death would be a symbolic sacrifice to demonstrate the cruelty and futility of capital punishment. Often he sounded like an adolescent infatuated with martyrdom. But at times, as in his last letter to one of his appeals attorneys, George T. Davis, Chessman rose to eloquence:

> Now my long struggle is over—yours isn't. This barbarous, senseless practice, capital punishment, will continue. In our society other men will go on taking that last walk to death until . . . when? Until the citizens of this state and this land are made aware of its futility. Until they realize that retributive justice is not justice at all.
>
> I die with the burning hope that my case and my death will contribute to this awareness, this realization. I know that you will personally do all in your power, as citizen and lawyer, to convince your fellows that justice is not served, but confounded, by vengeance and executions.

Nonetheless, in his books Chessman was not an effective opponent of capital punishment. In his second book, *Trial by Ordeal*, he gave great attention to the death penalty as an evil in society. But his overly theoretical discussion did not receive applause from the critics. His arguments were judged shallow and amateurish. In his third book, *The Face of Justice*, Chessman stayed far away from theory and went back to complaints about how the State had treated him. This was the formula that had succeeded so well in his first book, *Cell 2455, Death Row*. It was only during his last days, when his case attracted a number of foreign journalists, some seeking an emotional story, others out to reinforce their anti-American views, that Chessman went back to his general condemnation of capital punishment. His fourth-estate audience loved it and he heaped it on.

Even though it is plausible to doubt the sincerity of Chessman in his opposition to capital punishment in general, it is hard to condemn him for this. It is psychologically understandable that anyone would rather present himself as being punished for upholding a cause and thus in prison due to the fault of the state rather than for his own personal fault. Indeed, in the 1970s it has become common for prisoners convicted of ordinary crimes to refer to themselves as political prisoners, as for instance during the disorders in the prison at Attica, New York. Chessman never claimed he was a political prisoner, but there is a parallel to that idea in his insistence that the authorities wanted to execute him not so much for his crimes as to affirm their authority. Sad to say, the case gives some credence to his claim. There is a disturbing tone of personal animus against Chessman on the part of some of the authorities involved in the case. Chessman was not altogether off base in his contention that he was a martyr for the cause of capital punishment. However, as a martyr, it is necessary to believe in the cause. This forced Chessman to defend the abolition of capital punishment for everyone, not just himself.

In the long run, it was not a wise decision for Chessman to attempt to link his case with the capital punishment issue. It divided his efforts. He kept hopping back and forth, proclaiming his innocence, claiming his trial was unfair, and cheerleading opposition to the death penalty. The line of demarcation between these three issues became confused. A weakness in the assertions of Chessman and his supporters on any one of these issues lost points for him on the other two issues as well. More importantly, the general question of the suitability of capital punishment in a civilized society is so vital that the other issues in the case were overshadowed by it and practically disappeared from view.

Many of the supporters of Chessman argued that no one should be executed, not even Chessman. The phrasing of this line of attack led defenders of capital punishment to argue not only that there were indeed instances in which the death penalty was justified, but that Chessman's case was such an instance. To defend capital punishment, it became necessary for many people to insist that Chessman's sentence was completely justified. This neatly sidestepped key issues—whether Chessman was the "red light bandit," and whether he was found guilty beyond a reasonable doubt at a fair trial.

It is not surprising that Chessman enjoyed the notoriety, fame, and financial contributions that went along with being the fair-haired boy of the opponents of capital punishment. Unfortunately, not all those who rushed to his aid had the purest of motives, or were the most desirable of allies. A world-wide assortment of communist, socialist and leftist groups took up the case as the perfect opportunity to create anti-American sentiment. The effect that this type of support produced on the conservatively inclined forces of law enforcement in California can be imagined.

For the purposes of this book, the question of the death penalty can be attacked from three different angles. The first is along the general line of inquiry, "Is capital punishment ever justifiable?" Clearly, a negative answer precludes the execution of Chessman. If one arrives at an affirmative answer for the first inquiry, then it is necessary to consider whether a true violation of the California Penal Code occurred, and whether anyone should be executed for violating this section at all. Another affirmative response forces us to be more specific. Should Caryl Whittier Chessman, convicted violator of California Penal Code Sec. 209 have been executed? If the answer to any of these inquiries is negative, the execution was unjust.

This is not the place to launch into a full discussion of the ethical and legal aspects of whether capital punishment is justified. Instead, let us take a look at some practical aspects of the problem. First, the fact is that it is not simply a matter of what is good law. Public opinion must support capital punishment if it is to be applied, or oppose it if it is to be abolished. During this century attitudes have been changeable. In 1948 and the years during which Chessman was appealing his sentence, popular sentiment generally supported capital punishment. Today, the issue is much less clear. It appears that there is more opposition to capital punishment than earlier and a lot of uncertainty. Some of the uncertainty arises from the ambiguity of the 1972 United States Supreme Court decision concerning the death penalty in the Furman case. The Court could not muster a majority to hold that the death penalty was inherently such "cruel and unusual punishment" as to be prohibited by the Eighth Amendment. But it did agree that when the death penalty was applied in an arbitrary and random way it violated the Eighth Amendment in practice. The effect has been to outlaw capital punishment, either in practice or by law, as in California. But this is an unstable situation. The fact that the Supreme Court was reluctant to go so far as to say that capital punishment is inherently cruel and unusual punishment reflects the grave doubts that exist in many quarters about the correctness of that argument.

In fact, it seems likely to me that more rigorous attitudes will return in the future. Capital punishment is in eclipse now only because by today's standards it seems to many to be too harsh, regardless of the crime. But a shift in popular sentiment might return us to the kind of hanging-tree mentality of past years. If there is such a shift in popular sentiment it would probably be reflected in the courts. But if that does not happen, a second and clear possibility is that the Constitution could be amended to permit capital punishment even though it might be defined as cruel and unusual punishment. It is certainly true that legislative views might be changed or strengthened in the near future, perhaps by accidental events. Let one airplane hijacker toss a grenade killing 200 people in a 747 jet, or let one Congressman have his child die from a drug overdose, and there will be a rush for a return to the death penalty. Capital punishment is not yet a closed issue.

Supporters of capital punishment say that it is a just punishment for and the only possible deterrent to particularly horrid crimes. The examples of horrid crimes are varied: big-time drug dealing; murder for thrills (the "family" of Charles Manson is currently being cited here); assassinations of public figures; bombings; and airplane hijacking, especially where violence is used. The community, they say, must be protected from crimes such as these, and the death penalty provides the means by making the price so high that people will not take the risk. Further, they say, it is indisputably just to hold the offender accountable for his acts in such a way that the punishment fits the crime—in the biblical phrase, an eye for an eye. Generally, people who hold these views brush aside the advice of psychiatrists that the only valid kind of punishment is that which will rehabilitate the criminal. They have a low view of the likelihood of rehabilitation of a person who has committed a capital crime. Practicality as well as justice is thus used to support the deterrence argument.

There can be no doubt today that the death penalty is not an effective deterrent. Passion, liquor, lust, and greed all supercede it. Otherwise, killings would be on the decline, not the rise. Proponents of capital punishment would be better advised to avoid the deterrent argument and stick to those of just punishment and the unlikelihood of rehabilitation. But in many cases we can guess that the deterrence argument is a euphemism for getting even, or even for revenge. The desire that a criminal receive his "just deserts" is buried deep in the human heart. But people are uncomfortable with the idea of revenge and hide their real motivation behind the idea of deterrence.

A case is a deterrent only if the results lead others to say, "This will happen to me if I do the same thing." It is unlikely that anyone would say this after studying the Chessman case. What would be deduced is that it is crazy to defend oneself in such an arrogant manner. Since hardly anyone else would be capable of conducting such a prolonged, flamboyant attack on everything and everyone held sacred in the State of California, the case is not a good one to use as an example. Its deterrence factor is nil. If anything, all the publicity accorded Chessman could provoke just the opposite reaction from those with unbalanced mentalities. Proof of this is that on May 22, 1960, twenty days after Chessman's execution, three women, a doctor's wife, and a mother and her seventeen-year-old daughter, were raped and robbed in California by a "red light bandit."

The death of Caryl Chessman did not deter anyone from anything. Probably just the opposite. He stands as a symbol of prison defiance, revered in all the prisons of this land. The misdialed phone call by the secretary of Judge Goodman has become a legend, and in the legend the facts have been changed. The purpose of the call was not to grant a brief postponement for reading the latest defense plea; it was a call to free Chessman. The important point is that Chessman became a hero to the people who theoretically should have been frightened out of lives of crime by his execution. Anyone who ever spoke to a prison audience can affirm that prisoners know about Chessman and idealize him. Invariably one of the first questions from the audience concerns the unfair treatment accorded to their prison brother, Chessman.

It is impossible to say that Americans have arrived at the point where they permanently desire that no one ever should be executed again. Whether they should so desire is a question beyond the scope of this book. The best that can be said for the capital punishment issue as it pertains to Chessman is that, given the social climate of 1960, when he was actually executed, both sides achieved as much as could be expected. Advocates of capital punishment got their example upholding the principle of ultimate accountability for serious offenses against society. The opponents of capital punishment received international publicity for their views and picked up a martyr for their cause. The only one who did not gain was Caryl Chessman who died of cyanide gas.

11

Section 209

But talking about capital punishment in general does not take care of the Chessman case. We must turn to an examination of the section of the California penal code under which Chessman was sentenced to death, Sec. 209, to come to a better answer on the matter. Should anyone have been executed for violating it at all, and if so, did Chessman's acts warrant execution? California Sec. 209 is a provision of the kidnapping law which covers cases that involve not only kidnapping but certain other felonies as well, and which provides for stiffer sentences than ordinary kidnapping.

In 1948 Sec. 209 was a harsh and questionable section of the California kidnapping law. To understand the Chessman case we need to examine the general aspects of kidnapping law and then the specific application of Sec. 209 to Chessman.

Kidnapping is one of the most confusing and emotion-laden areas of the law. The definition of kidnapping is in itself difficult. For instance, what elements have to be present to call an act kidnapping: A ransom demand? Forced movement? Intent to kidnap? The Chessman case involved kidnapping charges even though no ransom was involved and so we must concentrate our attention on that type of kidnapping, generally called nonransom kidnapping. In almost all capital punishment states kidnapping is included among crimes other than murder which can carry the death penalty, although executions for crimes not involving murder are rare in all states. In California in 1948 the kind of kidnapping which carried the death penalty was the kind covered by Sec. 209; four men had been executed under its provisions since its adoption in 1933.

Section 209 was added to the California Penal Code in that year against the background of the violent public reaction to the kidnapping of the Lindbergh baby. The section has been modified by the California Legislature and by judicial interpretation since Chessman's conviction (as will be discussed later), but Chessman was convicted under the 1948 form of the law. The section deals with nonransom kidnapping where other felonies are directly involved. The first part of the section covered cases which involved both kidnapping and robbery, and carried only one sentence: life with the possibility of parole. For plain old ordinary kidnapping without robbery, the maximum sentence was twenty-five years, and often the sentence was less or the prisoner was paroled after ten or fifteen years. Thus, in practice, adding robbery to kidnapping increased the stakes significantly. The second provision raised them even more. It dealt with acts in which three things happened: kidnapping, robbery, and bodily harm to the victim. In this case, in Chessman's time, life without the possibility of parole was the minimum sentence and death was the maximum.

To appreciate the scope of California's Sec. 209 and to judge whether Chessman truly broke it, a discussion of the general nonransom kidnapping topic is most necessary. A comparison of the law in California with that in another populous and advanced state, New York, can help in this effort. The law in New York and California is not the same. What one state does will not bind the other. However, the differences in approach illustrate that no simple answer exists to nonransom kidnapping cases.

Until 1965, the New York law on nonransom kidnappings was fairly straightforward. Before that date, the most important case was the 1950 Florio case. Michael Florio climbed the stairs of a

Manhattan brownstone and rang the doorbell. He told a young girl who was visiting in the home that a friend of hers was in the waiting car. She knew none of the occupants but got in anyway. Against her will, she was driven to a remote spot in the neighboring borough of Queens. There the car was stopped and the four male occupants took turns raping her.

No money was involved in this case. There were no ransom notes, no protracted searches by grieved parents, no appearance by the FBI. The *Florio* case was a perfect example of a nonransom kidnapping. The girl was not raped at the steps of the brownstone. The attackers chose to drive her from the center of New York City to one of the outskirts. Anyone knowing how large New York City is will appreciate that this is far more than a trip around the corner. Added to the pain, fright, and suffering that the victim would naturally have suffered had she been raped immediately at the point of meeting is the added fear and terror that she must have suffered during this long forced ride. For this reason, in addition to a rape charge, New York authorities also charged the car occupants with kidnapping even though no money was involved. Kidnapping carries a stronger sentence in New York than rape. This seemed to be the best method open to the District Attorney to punish Florio and his companions for the extra suffering they caused their victim.

Legitimately, the point may be raised that the Florio crew had no intention of kidnapping their victim. One can almost hear their anguished cry—the reverse of that used by Chessman—"We are plain old rapists, man. Kidnapping ain't our bag." Nonetheless, the law has always been that no matter what your actual intention in an action-type crime, you are responsible for the results of your actions. If the law that prohibits kidnapping is fairly drawn in such a manner that your actions qualify, you fit, no matter what your intention. It has to be this way. Otherwise all criminals would be able to maintain with impunity that they did not intend to commit the criminal action with which they have been charged.

The New York kidnapping statute was widely drawn. There was no requirement of a demand for money as in some other states. Forced movement was the key provision. The New York

Court of Appeals, the highest state court, reviewed, and upheld the *Florio* conviction. It went farther than that. It reviewed and approved decisions it had made in two earlier kidnapping cases. The first one they upheld was the 1931 *Hope* case where police had overtaken and captured the criminal after he had only held his victim long enough to drive him one mile in an auto. They also approved the kidnapping conviction in the 1937 *Small* case, even though the time the victim was held did not exceed one minute. Small made the mistake of allowing the victim to drive the car himself. Showing quick wits, the victim smashed the car into the first traffic light he passed. Arrest for the surprised criminal was almost instantaneous.

The *Hope* and *Small* cases have in common the fact that no possible crime other than kidnapping appears from the circumstances. It was from no lack of trying on the part of these criminals that their kidnapping attempts ended so abruptly. The New York Supreme Court was applying strictly the theory of responsibility for one's actions. Adding these cases to the decision in *Florio*, it is possible to arrive at a rule for New York in 1950. If no motive other than kidnapping is discernible from your actions, kidnapping will be found. In the same manner, if substantial movement was over and above that connected with the underlying felony (e.g., robbery or rape), kidnapping will be found. It should be remembered that in New York, kidnapping carried a possible sentence of death. But this penalty virtually never was utilized. The alternative of life imprisonment was a sufficiently strong substitute.

Thanks to *Florio*, *Hope*, and *Small*, New York district attorneys had a clear guide concerning those cases in which they sought to press kidnapping charges to punish extra forced movement. But, in 1965, all this changed when the New York Court of Appeals handed down its decision throwing out kidnapping convictions in the *Levy* case. Adding insult to injury, the Court of Appeals used *Levy* as a vehicle to review and abandon their earlier holding in *Florio*. From now on, no one could use the facts of the Florio case to justify a kidnapping conviction in a new case. However, the Court of Appeals said that *Hope* and *Small* were still good law. Shocked lawyers and lower court judges dug themselves out of the debris and tried to figure why the roof had fallen and what was the extent of the damage.

The *Levy* decision can be summarized briefly. A wealthy member of the Mosler Safe Company family and his wife drove up to their Park Avenue apartment house. As they attempted to alight, Levy and his companion, who had been lurking in the shadows, forced the couple back into their car. During the next twenty minutes, they took the earrings and two finger rings worn by Mrs. Mosler and $300 from her husband. The total length of the forced ride was twenty-seven city blocks. The couple was released unharmed.

Although in *Levy* the trip was not as long as the one in *Florio*, conventional thinking would expect that the Court of Appeals would uphold the kidnapping conviction for the same reason that it had in *Florio*. The offense to the victims was more than would be adequately punished merely by a conviction for the underlying felony, in this case, robbery. It would seem that a criminal act over and above the robbery occurred. True, ransom was not the purpose. However, every other detail conformed to the standard kidnapping definition. By the act of throwing out the kidnapping conviction in *Levy* and saying that if another case with a fact pattern like *Florio* occurred, they would not sustain a kidnapping conviction, the court made a radical change in New York law.

In its opinion, the court said that *Levy* and *Florio* lacked "a true kidnapping flavor." In other words, in the eyes of the Court of Appeals, these were really robbery and rape, respectively, not kidnapping. The considerable movement in both cases did not change their opinion of the basic nature of these cases. This being so, they found it wrong for these criminals to receive the stiffer sentences meted out to kidnappers. The criminals should have been convicted and punished only for robbery and rape, respectively, according to the Court of Appeals.

If *Florio* and *Levy* can no longer be considered as kidnapping, the first question that arises is: Will any future case in New York without a ransom demand be considered as kidnapping? The Court of Appeals decision in *Levy* contains the answer. It is an affirmative one. At the same time that the *Levy* decision shot down *Florio*, the judges voiced their determination to continue

considering *Hope* and *Small* as good law in New York. No
ransom was involved in either case. The time between seizure of
the victim and capture was too short to establish any motive. A
short-lived kidnapping is all that appears on the record. Since
Hope and *Small*, two nonransom kidnapping cases, still would be
followed in New York, *Levy* did not mean that there would be no
such thing as a nonransom kidnapping in New York. If on the
facts of the case nothing other than kidnapping occurred, this
felony, with its stiff penalties, will be found even though the time
and distance of forced movement is short.

But could there be a nonransom kidnapping conviction in any
case in which there was also a conviction for another serious
felony? The Court of Appeals said yes. Neither *Levy* nor *Florio*
was such a case, but in appropriate cases, as for example *People*
v. *Black*, the court would sustain a nonransom kidnapping
conviction in addition to convictions for other felonies in the case.
This sent everyone on a mad dash to read the *Black* case to find
out how aggravated the circumstances would have to be in order
to sustain convictions for both the underlying felonies and a
nonransom kidnapping. The answer gave nightmares to the critics
of the Levy decision.

Reuben W. Black, a sometimes-employed handyman, broke
into the Long Island house of one of his customers. Then, he shot
the husband twice in the head as he lay sleeping in his bed. On
hearing the shots, the pregnant wife appeared from another room
in the house. Black fired at her from point-blank range, but
inexplicably missed. He tore out the telephone wire and bound
the badly wounded man with the wire. He burglarized the room.
Then he forced the woman to accompany him in his escape in the
family's car. He ignored her pleas to be allowed to telephone a
doctor for the husband or telephone for someone to care for her
infant sleeping in the crib. He was captured with his hostage a
couple of hours later in the next state after a high-speed chase by
state troopers. Cases like *Black* mercifully are rare. How much
short of *Black* would the Court of Appeals be willing to stop
while still being satisfied that both a nonransom-type kidnapping
and another felony occurred? *Levy* critics feared that the answer
would be—not very far. *People* v. *Lombardi*, the next case of this

sort decided by the New York Court of Appeals, proved the critics correct.

Lombardi was a travel agent and a licensed pharmacist. He ran both businesses from his Manhattan store. On three different occasions he asked female employees to accompany him to parties in Queens to help drum up travel agency business. Each time before entering his car, the girls took a "nail hardening pill" which he gave them, surely evidence that Lombardi was practiced in the art of persuasion. In reality, the pill was a sleep-inducing capsule of great potency. On each occasion, he drove the unfortunate employee to a motel in Queens. Sexual molestation, and, in one case, attempted rape occurred. The girls were under the effect of these pills from ten to fifteen hours, while remaining in Lombardi's custody. Lombardi diagnosed brittle nails for a fourth female employee. Unfortunately for him, this time his quail was an undercover policewoman.

The resemblances to the *Florio* case are quite striking. The deceptive proposal to get in the car was made in Manhattan. The car then drove from Manhattan to Queens. A sexual offense was the goal of the crime. However Florio and his pals neither drugged their victim nor kept her anywhere near a ten-hour period. The exaggerated means and perversity of the method to carry out the sexual attack in *Lombardi* would appear to put it in the same class of felonious movement that the Court of Appeals interdicted in *Black*.

The Court of Appeals fooled everyone and said no kidnapping. In a carelessly worded, shoddily reasoned opinion, the majority of the justices figuratively yawned and asked: "What is everyone so excited about; this is nothing but a friendly case of rape?" No one would have said anything if he had dragged the girls into the back of his drug store to rape them there. Why get upset that he chose to do it in Queens? Maybe he likes Queens. The ten to fifteen hours of utter helplessness in which Lombardi could have driven the victims half way to Florida if he so wished seemed to make no impression on the majority. The bitterly upset *Levy* critics were now ready to concede that the days of nonransom kidnapping were for all practical purposes finished in New York. They overestimated the consistency of the Court of Appeals. The next case of this type that came along went exactly in the opposite direction.

People v. *Miles* was, to say the least, a colorful case. Brooks, the victim, was a mentally defective, epileptic drifter. He had incurred the enmity of four criminals by disposing of a large shipment of heroin that they had left with him for safekeeping. In addition, Brooks had witnessed a murder committed by two of the four defendants. Obviously Brooks was in danger when he went to the Newark, New Jersey apartment of a girl member of the group to explain what happened to the heroin. The gang jumped Brooks and tried to kill him by injecting lye into his bloodstream. The homemade hypodermic needle employed failed to do the job. They gagged and tied him and set off for a deserted stretch of swampland known as the Jersey Meadows. Brooks was removed from the car and liberally doused with gasoline. Before they had the opportunity to light the match, a group of pedestrians walked close enough to the car that it was thought wiser to abandon the effort. Brooks, unconscious, still tied and now soaked with gasoline, was shoved into the car trunk. The next stop was Harlem in upper Manhattan where the four criminals adjourned to a bar to figure out their next move. Brooks had regained consciousness sometime during the interstate trip from New Jersey. He started to bang on the trunk cover from the inside. A passing policeman heard the thumping and investigated. The four villains were swiftly apprehended. The New York Court of Appeals majority listened to the facts, nodded their heads sagely—and called it a kidnapping!

People v. *Miles* was a true kidnapping case according to the justices because it was an extended trip, a complicated method of transportation, a change of purpose occurred, and the trip was not directly connected with trying to kill Brooks. All of this is true, undoubtedly. The problem is that virtually each of these three reasons could have been used to sustain a kidnapping conviction in *Lombardi*. There seems to be little difference between the two cases. This commentator is of the opinion that the *Miles* decision was correct, but not for the reason advanced. The justices forgot that all the actions enumerated took place in New Jersey except for capture. A New York court can punish only crimes committed in New York. Miles and his companions committed a whole raft of crimes against Federal and New Jersey statutes, but not against New York statutes. As far as New York is concerned, this is the same kind of kidnapping as in *Hope* or *Small*. Nothing other than kidnapping occurred in New York. Who knows what would have happened if the crew had been able to finish their beers, make new plans and return to deal with Brooks. The fact remains they didn't. Everything that happened before crossing the George Washington Bridge should have been a dead letter to New York. The right answer was reached for the wrong reason.

The New York Court of Appeals' batting average in nonransom kidnapping cases was low by the late 1960s. It was utterly impossible to guess whether the Court of Appeals would affirm a kidnapping conviction in a nonransom case or not. Any criminal with a little daring could well take his rape or robbery victim for a long ride and pick a nice safe spot to complete the desired action. As long as he didn't shoot the victim's husband in the head or try to stick a little lye in the victim's bloodstream, the chances that his excursion would cause extra punishment were very slight. It was a disgraceful situation. Instead of interpreting the statute, as is their function, the Court of Appeals had chosen to play legislators. Evenhanded administration of justice suffers whenever this occurs. The authorities charged with bringing to trial citizens who break the law as written must be able to rely on the law as written being applied by the courts. When judges play legislators, anything can happen; all the work expended to convict for kidnapping goes down the drain. If the law is defective, the remedy is for the state legislature to change the law.

The New York kidnapping law underwent radical revision in 1967. It would be pleasant to say that a brand new day dawned for New York with the change in its kidnapping statute. It is still too early to say definitively, but this does not seem to be true. Courts are slow. Since the law only applies to crimes committed after September 1, 1967, nothing on this matter could possibly reach the Court of Appeals until these cases had been investigated, prosecuted, convictions for kidnapping obtained, appeal denied by the intermediate court, and permission for review granted by the Court of Appeals. In addition, to see the effect of the new law we must allow time for attorneys to try out various theories under the new law, testing them on a case-by-case basis. Anything less than a ten-year shakedown cruise is too short for a valid judgment on the new New York kidnapping statute.

The New York Criminal Code received only piecemeal revision from its adoption in 1829 until 1967. One document can be patched only so many times. Time for a modern code had clearly come. Drafting laws prohibiting all the various ways that one man can impinge improperly on the rights of others in the community is a herculean task. Each separate crime cannot be given the individual theoretical attention that it deserves. Clearly, the kidnapping statute did not get sufficient attention. The drafters had good intentions. They saw merit in both sides of the *Levy* controversy. On one hand, they noted that what really is not kidnapping should not be punished as kidnapping. On the other hand, they recognized that something above the underlying felony of rape or robbery occurred when there was forced movement. They also were in accord that nonransom kidnappings in the true sense were possible. They tried to fit all possible types of false imprisonment into one statute with six different subdivisions. A large number of legal commentators think that they failed miserably and further confused an already impossible situation. Their faulty drafting managed the almost incredible feat of preserving most of the deficiencies of the old New York approach and, in one fell swoop, adding all the difficulties of the California approach—difficulties that Knowles and Chessman had brought into the California daylight.

Because of the Knowles and Chessman cases, California had to face some of the sticky problems of nonransom kidnappings fifteen years before New York's *Levy* case. In 1950 the nonransom kidnapping conviction of Chessman reached the California Supreme Court. The Court did not pull any punches: "It is the fact, not the distance, of forcible removal which constitutes kidnapping in this state." Therefore as early as 1950 the California courts had shown that the number of feet or number of minutes involved did not matter much; as long as forcible removal occurred, they were going to find kidnapping in a nonransom situation—without becoming human adding machines like the New York courts.

It should not have been difficult to figure out that the California Supreme Court was going to make a strict decision on the nonransom kidnappings in the *Chessman* case. Anyone who had followed the thinking of this court through the years could see that they were headed in this direction. In the 1935 *Raucho* case, forcing a victim to cross a street and enter an automobile had been enough for nonransom kidnapping. The same answer was given for dragging a victim from a sidewalk into a neighboring house in the 1937 *Cook* case, for a forced march of fifty to seventy-five feet in the 1938 *Melendez* case, and for carrying a child from the front of the house up onto the roof in the 1947 *Shields* case.

Chessman was charged with four different nonransom kidnappings: Mary Alice Meza, Regina Johnson, and the two clothing store men at Redondo Beach, Melvin Waisler and Joe Lescher. In the Mary Alice Meza case, a two-hour drive around the streets of Los Angeles was involved. There is no doubt from the pre-1950 California cases on the subject that for Mary Alice there had been more than enough movement to qualify as nonransom kidnapping in California. In fact, had the Chessman case been tried in New York courts, one can judge from the contemporaneous *Florio* case, that it would have been found a clear case of nonransom kidnapping. The fact that New York later changed its approach and, by 1965, said that *Florio* should only have been a rape case and not a nonransom kidnapping would be of little consolation to the already dead Chessman. By 1948 standards, the movement requirements for nonransom kidnapping in either state would have been satisfied in the Meza case. Unfortunately, the movement in the Meza case may not hold up much longer because California can hardly avoid going along with the tendency to loosen kidnapping movement requirements. It seems to me, however, that the case *should* hold up because the flavor of kidnapping would seem strong enough in this case to satisfy any reasonable man's taste, no matter how strong his preference might be.

As to Mrs. Johnson, the answer is not so automatic. The distance involved was twenty-two feet. The forced detention was ten minutes, and it was a different sort of detention than for Meza. Compared to the earlier California cases (*Raucho*, *Cook*, *Melendez* and *Shields*), the movement in the Johnson case is little, if any, shorter in distance than those and probably a little longer in temporal duration. If Chessman had had Mrs. Johnson march the ten minutes in question rather than spend most of it in the Ford, the distance involved would have been at least one third of a mile. On the other hand, presumably the time in the Ford was spent in the act of oral intercourse and, thus, should be merged with the unnatural sex act offense and not be considered part of the time for the nonransom kidnapping. Whether the Johnson case was a nonransom kidnapping is a close question. Mostly thanks to the verbal raspberries that Chessman kept giving to the court, he won no such close questions.

On the whole, it would seem that the movement part of the Johnson case would also have qualified as kidnapping by California standards of that period. Would it have been nonransom kidnapping by 1948 New York standards? The answer might very possibly be no. Wisely, New York was much more reluctant to charge kidnapping in what was essentially a rape or robbery case than was California. In a broader comparison, we may say that while it would take the 1965 *Levy* decision to rule out a Meza-type kidnapping conviction in New York, a Johnson-type kidnapping conviction most probably could never have been obtained in New York.

The doubts raised about there being sufficient movement to charge kidnapping in the Johnson case are even stronger in the two charges of kidnapping in the Redondo Beach robberies. New York never would have claimed that the truly incidental movement of the clothiers from the showroom into the back of the store was a kidnapping-type movement. California never should have done so either. This was extending to the breaking point the California idea that the amount of movement involved did not matter in a nonransom kidnapping. Another point is that it was not even Chessman who did the moving of the victims. It was Knowles. True, an accomplice at a crime is legally as responsible as the principal. However, when the act of movement itself is virtually nonexistent, to go a step further and hold the accomplice responsible for kidnapping is absurd.

The California kidnapping statute of the Chessman days was badly drawn. It was so worded that no movement was needed at all in order to qualify as kidnapping. Mere detention technically was enough. Thus in reality, every robbery, rape, or assault could technically have been considered a kidnapping since some detention occurs of necessity in all of these crimes. A bloodthirsty prosecutor could tack on a kidnapping charge any time he wished. Unbelievable as it seems, until 1960, a poor sucker could be found guilty of two crimes in California for what really was the same act and serve double sentences. In 1960, California eliminated this unjust possibility of double conviction and punishment by modifying the law to the extent that the criminal must serve only the sentence for the crime that he intended to commit.

The California Supreme Court upheld the kidnapping convictions of both Chessman and Knowles when their cases made their separate ways to the high court for review in 1950. However, in the *Knowles* case they recommended to the Legislature that it think about changing the definition of kidnapping. The next year, the Legislature did so. From 1951 movement as well as detention was required to qualify as kidnapping. After this change of the law, at least some little movement would have to occur in order to charge kidnapping. While there was some little movement at Redondo Beach and thus in theory it could still be called kidnapping, even by 1960 standards, it simply wasn't kidnapping. It was first degree robbery and assault with a deadly weapon, pure and simple. The Los Angeles District Attorney's office should never have brought the charge. It should not have used the Redondo Beach robbery to reinforce the case for a death penalty for Chessman.

It took the California Supreme Court eighteen years to get around to setting down guidelines as to how much movement was necessary to constitute kidnapping according to the 1951 amendment to the statute. In 1969, the *Daniels* case said that seventy-five feet of movement in a rape situation was not enough for a conviction of kidnapping. Since then the California Supreme Court has followed this line of reasoning in a whole group of cases: no kidnapping when the victims were pistol whipped into crawling into the adjacent room during a robbery (*Mutch*); no kidnapping when the victim was driven five city blocks during a robbery (*Timmons*); no kidnapping in movement of supermarket employees from check stand and manager's office to a safe (*Ungrad*); no kidnapping when a jeweler and companion were moved from room to room during a robbery (*Killian*); no kidnapping when a hotel night clerk was moved to the second floor during a robbery (*Smith*); no kidnapping when liquor store employees were moved into a back storage area during a robbery and a gas station employee was forced to lie down on the lube room floor (*Adams*); no kidnapping when victims were forced to take a robber on a tour of their house (*Hunter*); no kidnapping when a robbery-rape victim was moved across the livingroom and into the bedroom (*Norman*); no kidnapping when the robbery victim was forced to move up and down the stairs of his private house (*Morrison*).

The California Supreme Court threw out kidnapping in each instance because the forced movement was merely incidental to the robbery or rape and not a separate act. In effect the California Supreme Court is using the same criteria as the New York Court of Appeals did in *Levy*. Was the flavor of kidnapping present in these movement situations? It should be noted that the distances involved in these 1969-1971 California cases are much shorter than the distances faced in such cases as *Florio*, *Lombardi*, or *Levy* in New York. (See Charts 1 and 2). It is most probable that even today California still would be inclined to find sufficient movement for kidnapping if faced with any of these New York situations. At least to the present, the flavor of kidnapping is not identical in the two states. This statement presumes that the new statute in New York is capable of flavoring anything. Many people think it unwittingly permits standstill kidnapping in New York—a trap the Empire State never fell into even in its most confused days in the past.

Now let us turn to the question of Chessman's convictions for kidnapping. If the acts in question had been committed after the

CHART 1 New York Kidnapping Cases

Case	Year	Distance*	Time*	Other Felony**	Kidnapping
Hope	1931	1 mile by car	3 min.	———	yes
Small	1937	600 yds. by car	1 min.	———	yes
Florio	1950	20 miles by car	3 hrs.	rape	yes until 1965; then no
Black	1962	out of state by car, 50 miles	4½ hrs.	attempted murder, assault with a deadly weapon, robbery	yes
Levy	1965	28 blocks by car	20 min.	robbery	no
Lombardi	1967	20 miles by car	10 to 15 hrs.	sexual molestation, attempted rape	no
Miles	1967	into state by car, 20 miles	4½ hrs.	not in N. Y.	yes

*Approximation by author
**Generalization of charges

CHART 2 California Kidnapping Cases

Case	Year	Distance*	Time*	Other Felony**	Kidnapping 209
Raucho	1935	30 ft.	2 min.	rape	yes
Cook	1937	50 ft.	3 min.	rape	yes
Melendez	1938	65 ft.	4 min.	no	yes
Shields	1945	30 ft.	2 min.	no	yes
Oganosoff	1947	20 ft.	2 min.	robbery	yes
Knowles	1950	10 ft.	2 min.	robbery and assault	yes
Chessman	1950	10 ft.	2 min.	(Redondo Beach) robbery	yes
Chessman		22 ft.	10 min.	(Johnson) rape	yes
Chessman		40 miles by car	2 hrs.	(Meza) rape	yes
Langdon	1959	40 ft.	3 min.	rape and robbery	yes
Daniels	1969	75 ft.	10 min.	rape and robbery	no
Mutch	1971	15 ft.	5 min.	robbery	no
Timmons	1971	5 city blocks by car	5 min.	robbery	no
Ungrad	1971	20 ft.	5 min.	robbery	no
Killian	1971	15 ft.	5 min.	robbery	no
Smith	1971	50 ft.	5 min.	robbery	no
Adams	1971	20 ft. and 2 ft.	5 min. and 1 min.	robbery	no
Hunter	1971	300 yards	5 min.	robbery	no
Norman	1971	60 ft.	5 min.	robbery and rape	no
Morrison	1971	200 ft.	8 min.	robbery	no

*Approximation by author
**Generalization of charges

1969 California Supreme Court decision, how would the Court interpret the movement in his cases? The list of cases recently decided would seem to make the answer in all but the Meza case quite clear—no kidnapping. The movement for Mrs. Johnson, Melvin Waisler, and Joe Lescher does not qualify by present-day California standards. There is not enough movement. It would still be possible to charge Chessman with the underlying felonies of first degree robbery, assault with a deadly weapon, and unnatural sex acts. But the point here is to show how slender was the basis of the kidnapping convictions on three charges. This fundamental change in the California approach within nine years of Chessman's death must raise disquieting thoughts about the state's stiff-necked position earlier.

This is so even though the court in *Daniels* remarked the Chessman case would be decided in the same manner today. Most commentators discounted this as a self-serving declaration hiding the fact that people had been executed because of the statute interpretation the court now found unsound.

But forced movement alone never risked the death penalty in California. According to California law, you could drive someone from the redwood forest to Dead Man's Valley and back seven times without incurring the death penalty. Only if one moved across state lines, would the possibility of a death penalty exist. A demand for ransom in a California kidnapping also did not bring the death penalty. In the statute, life imprisonment is the maximum sentence provided. Chessman fell into a large hole. Professional kidnappers do not get executed in California. He, an amateur, without a thought of kidnapping in his head, did. How did this state of affairs come about? That brings us back to Sec. 209.

Under Sec. 209 a death sentence was possible when kidnapping, robbery and bodily harm to the victim were combined in one act. The jury found Chessman guilty of kidnapping, robbing, and causing bodily harm to Regina Johnson and Mary Alice Meza and applied the maximum sentence—death. But it also found Chessman guilty of exactly the same offense in connection with the Redondo Beach clothiers, but did not call for the maximum sentence. One can surmise that the jury was dubious of the prosecution's motives in bringing this Sec. 209 charge against Chessman. It is to their credit that the jurors did not try to bolster the two death penalty recommendations with two others in hopes a court reviewing the case might be overwhelmed.

The heart of the Sec. 209 charge is the requirement that kidnapping be combined with robbery and, in the case of the second part of the provision, with bodily harm. The Redondo Beach case is very straightforward in this respect. Three hundred dollars and clothes were taken from the Redondo Beach clothing store. In addition, Waisler was pistol-whipped by Knowles. Chessman, as his companion, is legally as much to blame as if he had done the pistol-whipping. No doubt, robbery and bodily harm occurred. Everything is present here except clear forced movement. Today, these Sec. 209 convictions would fall on the movement question, although the other ingredients still would be present. First degree robbery and assault with a deadly weapon would be chargeable.

The Johnson case posed no difficulties in meeting the robbery requirements of 1948-era California courts nor would it today. Five dollars were taken from Mrs. Johnson's purse immediately after the attack in the Ford. Bodily harm clearly existed in the sex attack unless one believes the Machlin-Woodfield theory that her failure to give explicit details at the first recounting of the incident to police meant that the incident never occurred. On even the slightest chance that this was true, the death penalty should not have been passed. If it was not absolutely certain that bodily harm had occurred, the provision of Sec. 209 which carried the death penalty would not have applied. That does not mean that a Sec. 209 kidnapping charge could not have been sustained, but it does mean that the maximum possible sentence would have been life imprisonment with the possibility of parole. Of course, while the unnatural sex acts and first degree robbery convictions in the Johnson case could still stand today, the twenty-two feet of movement and ten minutes of detention involved simply would not be enough for a Sec. 209 charge today.

The one case where the movement was substantial is paradoxically the only one of the four in which the robbery element is doubtful. Mary Alice Meza threw her pocketbook into the back of her companion's car when the "red light bandit" approached. Therefore she never was robbed. Actually it is impossible to know whether a real money demand was even made of her. What does "Let me have your money" mean? Does it mean only the money of the man in the car, Hurlburt, or the money of both Hurlburt and Meza? The question is crucial. If only Hurlburt's money was demanded, then there was no attempt to rob Mary Alice; and thus, an essential element of any Sec. 209 charge fails and Chessman should not have been condemned to death. This would be true, no matter what year the event occurred.

Even if it is assumed that there was a robbery demand of Mary Alice, two other difficulties remain. The statute says robbery; it does not say attempted robbery. The reviewing courts justified including attempted robbery in this case on the theory that Chessman should not be rewarded because Mary Alice's purse was empty. They assumed that if Mary Alice had been carrying money, the attacker would have taken it. On this sort of reasoning, a man who puts five bullets into someone with a sufficiently healthy constitution to survive the attack, could still be executed under a first degree murder statute on the theory that his victim lived despite the clear intention to commit first degree murder. All of this shows the questionable statute-stretching that was done in the Chessman case. It is hard to see how, on one hand, a court can say that you kidnapped her even though you didn't intend to do so, and on the other hand, say even though she had no money you robbed her for statute purposes because you intended to do so. The logic of this position is most cloudy.

The second grave difficulty with the robbery part of the Meza Sec. 209 conviction has to do with the timing. Any possible robbery demand made on Mary Alice occurred while she was still in Hurlburt's car. Can it be said that the robbery was part and parcel of the kidnapping attempted rape, and unnatural sexual actions? It is at least arguable that the robbery attempt was a completed action before the other offenses occurred. According to this theory, Chessman could be charged separately with robbery, and also with ordinary non-Sec. 209 kidnapping, attempted rape and committing unnatural sex acts. However, it would not be possible to claim they were one continuing action for the purposes of Sec. 209. Therefore, Sec. 209 with its possible death sentence could not be charged.

The main point behind this reasoning, which was used by Chessman, is that the intention of the bandit was robbery. The other crimes were an afterthought conceived when the robbery was thwarted by the victim's lack of money. Considering general judicial attitudes toward Chessman, it is not surprising that this subtle argument did not get much of a hearing. The judges found sufficiently close temporal connection to justify considering the whole affair as one related action covered by the stringent Sec. 209 provisions. The possible intentions of the attacker never bothered them. Probably they are correct. The Chessman theory demands too much reliance on the pre-existing intentions of Chessman. It is hard to know what he was thinking. This counts against him when it is remembered that a criminal normally is responsible for the results of his actions, regardless of subjective intentions. The intention argument is a close question. This is one time Chessman properly lost a close decision. Even so, it could have provided another justification for executive clemency. Governor Brown did not utilize it.

There seems to be little question that bodily harm occurred to Mary Alice. Her frantic emotional state and the subsequent medical examination both confirm this. Because descriptions of the attack were not furnished in her first interview with police, Machlin and Woodfield naturally say no real attack occurred. When the age and inexperience of Mary Alice are considered, the same justification used to excuse this lack of detail in the Johnson attack applies here as well with even more vigor. Even if by some chance an unnatural sex action did not occur in the Meza case, attempted rape did. This also fulfills the Sec. 209 bodily harm criteria. The only other possible explanation would be the start of sexual relations with her companion, and absolutely nothing supports this view. Bodily harm by the attacker certainly occurred in the Meza case. But it does not seem enough for a Sec. 209 conviction carrying the death penalty.

Thus, in one way or another, all four of the Sec. 209 convictions against Chessman would be likely to fail if they came up for consideration today, and the grounds on which to execute him would have evaporated. In fact, in retrospect, it can be seen that while Chessman was officially condemned to death because he was a kidnapper, the technical reason is only a pretense. In reality it was because he was an arrogant young man who forced two women to place his penis in their mouths for his sexual gratification. The starkness of this description is justified. Virtually every authority commenting on the Chessman case termed him a degenerate person, a sexual pervert, suggesting that in some way he seemed dangerous to society because of sexual deviancy.

In fact, even by 1948 standards, it is not clear that Chessman was sexually deviant. The evidence shows that the real intention in the two cases was to commit rape. Since the oral intercourse was resorted to as an alternative because these women were menstruating, it is only fair for the purposes of this analysis to consider the attempts at forced oral intercourse as part and parcel of the attempts at rape and not as separate sexual offenses. It is most likely that if the women were not menstruating there would have been no acts of oral intercourse. The original intention to commit rape would have been fulfilled, instead. One doubts that the death sentence would have been pronounced then, and even if it had been pronounced, one doubts the sentence would have been carried out.

Before the execution of Chessman, four other men had been executed in California for Sec. 209 kidnapping. In May, 1936, Thomas Edward Dugger was hanged for robbing, raping and brutally beating three women. Later the same year, Joseph Kristy and Alexander McKay were hanged for throwing a parole board member hostage out of a moving car during the unsuccessful prison break. As a result of his injury the victim had to have his leg amputated. On February 11, 1955, John Richard Jensen, twenty-nine, was gassed to death at San Quentin for sodomizing and burying alive a young Marine hitchhiker. All four of these men displayed a wanton disregard for the life of their victims. It was strictly luck and with no assistance of the criminal that these victims did not die.

In the eighteen felonies with which Chessman was charged, no such wanton disregard of the lives of others can be found. He fired no shots; he beat no one; he strangled no one. The one victim that was transported from the crime scene, Mary Alice Meza, was driven to the vicinity of her home. Even though robbery, sexual molestation, and Sec. 209 kidnapping occurred, none of the brutal disrespect for the lives of others that appears in all the other execution cases can be found in the Chessman case.

In these circumstances the charge that Mary Alice Meza ended up as a mental case at Camarillo State Hospital because of the Chessman attack takes on great importance. If true, it is much easier to place Chessman in the reckless-disregard-of-life category shared by the other four nonmurderer executees. The opponents of Chessman came up with the slogan: "He didn't take a life, he took a mind." Judge Fricke, Prosecutor Leavy and other public figures gave support to this theory. The committing psychiatrist, George N. Thompson, M.D., Chief Psychiatrist, Los Angeles Superior Court, did not agree. He always stuck to his opinion that Mary Alice's schizophrenia has commenced long before the attack. According to Thompson, verifiable mental deterioration set in from the time she had a diseased thyroid at the age of twelve. Regardless of the Chessman attack, he maintained that she was doomed to hopeless insanity. Assuming the doctor was correct, Chessman does not belong in the same class with the four others executed.

The contrast between the sentence served by Chessman and that served by David Knowles is a further ironic demonstration that all the cards were stacked against the unlucky Chessman. By the time Chessman paid the supreme price, Knowles was a free man back on the street attempting to earn an honest living. He had been much luckier with Sec. 209 than Chessman. His case was the reason the Legislature altered the provision in 1951. Not only did it change the definition of kidnapping as discussed earlier, but it also changed the Sec. 209 minimum sentence for bodily harm (life imprisonment without parole) to allow parole. Knowles, who had been sentenced to life without the possibility of parole on his Sec. 209 charge arising out of the Redondo Beach affair, was the first man to benefit from the modification of Sec. 209 and was paroled after serving a fairly short sentence.

But the 1951 change in Sec. 209 did not affect the maximum

penalty, death, in cases involving bodily harm. It is odd that the Legislature retained the death penalty in Sec. 209, especially since the reason it gave for modifying the provision for life imprisonment without possibility of parole was that it was too harsh. While only three men had died under the provision by 1951 and all of these in 1936, it is hard to explain why the death penalty was not replaced by life imprisonment. It cannot be attributed to concern with Chessman since his case was not yet big news. But then it never made much sense to make a Sec. 209 kidnapping a death offense anyway, even considering the furor over the Lindbergh case. When blame is handed out for the Chessman situation, the California Legislature ought to receive its fair share.

Standing back from Sec. 209 in order to obtain perspective, one sees a poorly drafted, overly technical, monstrosity that, ironically, is cloudy in purpose. The Chessman crimes fitted its precepts in the same almost-but-not-quite manner as did the 5000 other criminal acts occurring in California during the past forty years. If his crimes were committed today, the emphasis would fall more upon the "not quite" part than upon the "almost."

Joe Kristy, Alexander McKay, Thomas Edward Dugger, John Richard Jensen, Caryl Chessman, and Bill Wesley Monk all have one thing in common. They were executed under Sec. 209. Why these six and not Edward Wesley Brown, Harold Jackson, Eddie Wein, Harold Langdon, Gene Daniels, Archie Simmons, Robert Emmet Thornton, Million L. McShane, and Gary Phoinix? These nine also came to Quentin to die via Sec. 209. None of them did and none of them will. The reasons for this group escaping are as diverse as the crimes they committed: commutation by the governor to life without parole; new trials resulting in sentences of life without parole (never acquittal); the abolition of the death penalty by the California Supreme Court; and, in one case (Harold Jackson), suicide. Clearly, the difference between the first Sec. 209 category and the second one is arbitrary. A look at the dates of Sec. 209 executions (three in 1936, one each in 1955, 1960, and 1961) supports this. Equally arbitrary are the reasons that separate these two categories of 209ers sentenced to death from the many hundreds of 209ers who crossed the portals of San Quentin sentenced only to life with or without possibility of parole.

The six 209ers executed since 1930 are part of a group of fourteen executed in California for crimes other than murder. No women have been executed for anything but murder. California Penal Code Section 4500 accounted for the other eight men. This statute is directed against violence by a life-termer. Joe Kristy and Alexander McKay who were executed under Sec. 209 could just as easily have been tried and executed under Sec. 4500 for their abortive 1935 San Quentin prison break. Stealing the warden's car and pushing a parole board member hostage out of the speeding auto fit either category. Until recently changed, it was so poorly drafted that one prisoner punching another during a yard scuffle theoretically would qualify because the courts in California had defined all those serving indeterminate sentences (that is, every felon whose sentence was other than life or execution) as lifers for the purpose of Sec. 4500. That unfair decision meant that each and every California felon stood in danger of falling afoul of Sec. 4500's death penalty provision. Thank goodness, the California Legislature recently tidied up Sec. 4500 to the point where the violence must be directed against a nonprisoner and the victim must die of the attack within a year. But it is still less than the best of statutes.

Eight men have been executed under the provisions of Sec. 4500 since 1930 (William Bagley, Ethan McNabb, Wilson De LaRoi, Louis Smith, John Allen, Harold Berry, Robert Harmon, and Rudolph Wright). This is disquieting, especially because the victims of attacks by Bagley, McNabb, and Harmon did not die. As with Sec. 209, many of the men sentenced to die for Sec. 4500 violations escaped the rope and the gas chamber. Specifically, of twenty-two men sentenced to death, fourteen were not executed. The reasons, generally speaking, are the same type as with Sec. 209, including one suicide. And as with Sec. 209 the irregularity with which the executions take place suggests random application: Two were executed in 1935, one each in 1946, and 1955, two in 1957, and again one each in 1960 and 1962.

In addition to the fourteen executions discussed above, in the last forty years California has carried out 280 executions for murder. The hit-or-miss pattern discernible in Sec. 209 and Sec. 4500 executions seems largely to apply to the murder executions. California's execution statistics are by no means as shocking as some others. Its total of 292 (according to *National Prisoner Statistics*, published by the United States Bureau of Prisons—my own count is 294) places it fourth behind Georgia (366), New York (329) and Texas (297) in total executions since 1930. The most shocking figure of all is that of Georgia, a relatively small state, which executed 298 blacks in this period. The significance of this is too clear to require explanation. But the point to make about California's executions is the arbitrariness. When the United States Supreme Court held that arbitrary application of the death penalty amounted to "cruel and unusual punishment," California must have been one of the states that led them to its decision.

The Supreme Court decision spurred on California to find a nonarbitrary capital punishment statute. First it was necessary to strike down the February 1972 California Supreme Court decision that found the death penalty to be unconstitutional on "cruel and unusual punishment" grounds. In November 1972, the voters authorized the legislature to enact a new death penalty bill. Within 10 months, Governor Reagan had signed such a bill. After signature date, the gas chamber will be mandatory for hired assassins, police killers, life-term convicts who slay guards, mass and repeated murderers, train wreckers, persons who commit rape, robbery, kidnapping, burglary and lewd acts involving children, and those who kill witnesses to crimes. As could be expected, the new law has been challenged as constitutionally over broad and this not enforceable. No one sentenced to death under the new law will be executed until the United States Supreme Court rules on the question.

Even if Chessman could be found guilty of violating Sec. 209 today, there is no way he could be executed, since it is not a death penalty offense under the new law. We have established that by 1974 standards only the Meza attack might qualify as a Sec. 209 violation. Even if it did, life without parole is the maximum sentence now possible. Liberal lawyers in California are lining up to challenge the constitutionality of the "without parole" feature of a sentence. They claim this decision should be in the hands of parole officials and not the judge or jury. They may win. The day may be coming when Sec. 209 will be so emasculated that even if a violation is obtained under post-*Daniels* structures, the offender can be back on the streets in a short number of years. Chessman and the other five men executed on Sec. 209 charges all happened into this world too soon for their own good.

Governor Brown and Executive Clemency

12

Let us move to the third part of our inquiry on Chessman and the death penalty: Should he actually have been executed once convicted? And that brings us to the question of executive clemency, and to Chessman's life during his years on Death Row. For the purposes of argument, assume all the following propositions: Chessman was the "red light bandit"; he was found guilty beyond a reasonable doubt at a fair trial; capital punishment was justifiable in midcentury America; Chessman violated section 209 and could properly be executed for it. Even after all these less than totally sure propositions are affirmed, one large question remains: Should Governor Edmund G. Brown have commuted his sentence to life imprisonment?

To give the impression that Pat Brown is the only man who could have exercised executive clemency in this case would be unfair. The Chessman controversy spanned the term of several California governors. Governor Earl Warren could have commuted the sentence to life imprisonment in 1948 at the time of the trial. Warren was the most liberal of all California governors on the clemency issue. Nevertheless, habitually, he waited until the week of execution before making a clemency decision. While there are no guidelines for a governor on whether and when to spare the life of a condemned criminal, Warren generally interpreted the requirement that justice be served on the side of clemency. Had he been governor at the crucial point in the Chessman case it seems plausible that he would have granted clemency. But it is unlikely that he ever considered the case because it was so early in the process, before the avenue of appeal had been exhausted. Warren's successor, Goodwin J. Knight, had a different view of the function of the governor in clemency decisions. He passed up many opportunities to commute Chessman's sentence in 1954.

> People seem to forget what Chessman did. People expect me to sit as a super Supreme Court. I am not supposed to sit here like a superman and decide which court was wrong. . . . Nobody said the law shouldn't apply to people who write books.

As should be no surprise, commutations in general were negligible during Goodie Knight's term.

In this country, last-minute commutations have become part of the whole sickening death-day ritual. Hot lines to the office of the governor fit right in with such other hypocritical practices as giving the condemned his choice for the last meal and permitting him his personal television set for the last week of his existence. Since commutation is a part of the legal process, there exists no reason why governors should not draw up classifications and guidelines for themselves when they first go into office. Each case could be decided well in advance. The prisoner would know whether the governor was likely to act or not. False hope would be eliminated. Warren and Knight cannot be criticized in this regard. They both had clearly defined personal guidelines and stuck to them. Political considerations were not totally absent, but in general, one knew where he stood. As to Pat Brown, the one thing that could be said for sure is that no one knew where he stood.

When the California Legislature prescribed execution as a possible penalty in Sec. 209 offenses, no necessity that the circumstances be aggravated was written into the statute. A jury

was free to return, and a trial judge to concur in, a Sec. 209 death
penalty when no reckless disregard of life occurred. This actually
happened a few times. In each case, the governor exercised his
power of clemency to commute the death sentence to life in
prison.

Governor Brown always avowed his abhorrence for the death
penalty. Shortly before the Chessman execution, he commuted
the sentence of Eddie Wein, "the want-ad rapist," who had been
convicted of twenty felonies including five separate Sec. 209
violations. Summing up in that case, Prosecutor J. Miller Leavy
had said that Wein was worse than Chessman. Brown also
commuted the conviction of Howard Langdon. Langdon had
struck and injured the young female who was his rape-robbery
victim. It can be pointed out that the lives of the victims were not
immediately threatened in either case, but that was also true in
Chessman's case.

Then Governor Brown called a special session of the California
Legislature to consider a proposal to abolish the death penalty in
California. The Legislature's Senate Judiciary Committee held
special hearings—it was here that J. Miller Leavy dropped his
bombshell about Barbara Graham's confession. In the end, the
Judiciary Committee evaded the issue, by voting not to report the
proposal to the full Legislature. That got the legislators off the
hook, but it just put Governor Brown back on it. He still had full
rights to grant clemency to Chessman. But he did not commute
the sentence. Apparently Brown, when he considered whether or
not to grant clemency, gave some weight to the argument that
Chessman had brought on Mary Alice Meza's insanity. But since,
as shown earlier, Dr. Thompson's professional opinion made the
argument dubious, it is possible to say that the asserted
nonrepentence of the arrogant Chessman was really the reason he
was not granted clemency and was executed. If Chessman
actually was denied commutation because of arrogance, this
would be the first time that a man was executed for this reason in
the long death-penalty history of California. Though the governor
had the right to deny Chessman clemency, his decision to do so
was a decided stiffening of the day-to-day rule of reason used in
that state for more than a quarter of a century to determine

which nonmurderers sentenced to death actually should be put to death.

Poor Pat Brown! He had jumped left; he had jumped right; he had pleaded and emoted; he had brought the legislators back for a special session; he had hidden behind the skirts of second-string U.S. State Department officials. Finally, he threw the ball to the California Supreme Court. It is true that court sits as a clemency board on commutation decisions involving previous felons. In reality, it merely rubber stamps the wishes of the governor. But Brown played the sphinx. He knew no matter what he recommended, a sizable portion of California voters would be mad at him. Brown was damned if he did and damned if he didn't. So, in true political fashion, he sat on his hands and did nothing. For this he should be damned most of all.

It is possible to make a case that Chessman repented during his twelve years on death row. It is possible to make a case that a twelve-year wait is, in and of itself, "cruel and unusual punishment." It is possible to make a case that the gravity of his offenses had been exaggerated and that he should not be executed for the crimes he actually committed. Pros and cons exist for all three arguments. A reasonable man could justifiably go either way on one or all. The point is that it does not seem Governor Brown arrived at his decision after considering these issues. His sole frame of reference seemed to be, "Will my decision hurt or help my political career?"

The legal side of the Chessman case may not be laudable. However, at least this can be said: for twelve years, personality conflicts notwithstanding, people tried to arrive at a decision based on the merits of the case. Then Brown, who was actively seeking the Democratic nomination for the vice-presidency, came along and chucked it into the political arena. If it hadn't already become a fiasco, he made it one.

If Pat Brown had considered the issues, should he have spared Chessman's life because he had repented on death row? Actually "repent" is probably not the right word since it has connotations of accepting one's guilt. Chessman maintained steadfastly that he had not committed any of the seventeen crimes for which he was convicted. Whether true or not, the constitutional guarantee against self-incrimination permits anyone, even a condemned man, to maintain his innocence. In one of the better-reasoned parts of George Jackson's collection of his prison letters, *Soledad Brother*, he points out the impossibility of obtaining parole unless one confesses to past crimes. His objection to this practice on constitutional grounds has some validity in theory. However, in practice it does not seem to me workable, since in the vast preponderance of instances the prisoner who denies having committed his crimes is lying. This objection can be made to the denials of culpability by Chessman. However, in his case, we are talking about only a sufficient amount of rehabilitation necessary to live in a prison community—not sufficient rehabilitation to permit his going back into the outside world for a long time, if ever. Since it is part of the prison code that every prisoner is there on a bum rap, framed by the crooked lawyer, judge, D.A., cop or wife—or all five together—maintaining his innocence should not be held against Chessman. It is a *sine qua non* of day-to-day prison existence.

If it is semantically incorrect to say that Chessman repented, can it be said that he rehabilitated himself while on Death Row? Of course reference is being made to the four books he published during this period: *Cell 2455, Death Row*; *Trial By Ordeal*; *The Face of Justice*; and the novel *The Kid Was A Killer*. Did his success as an author indicate rehabilitation? The answer is probably not. He tried to become an author before going to prison. He continued under more restricted conditions what he had begun when free. If a well-known author went to prison and wrote his tenth best seller on Death Row, no one would suggest this demonstrated repentence—rather it would show he had improved his skills in the certainty that there would be no more output to represent him. Much the same rationale exists for Chessman. Actually his books were little more than self-glorification. Any subject he dealt with failed once it got away from his favorite theme: "Look how tough I am." His writing was more like a story in a detective magazine than art. Had he lost his notoriety, he would have lost his reading public as well.

Still, this is secondary to the important question raised by the rehabilitation argument. To what extent should rehabilitation ameliorate assigned punishment? Many Death-Row prisoners are there for one mistake in an otherwise law-abiding life, say murder in the anger of a domestic quarrel or a drunken brawl. For the most part, the notion of rehabilitation really does not apply to such cases where the crime was a single mistaken act. Should Chessman, a habitual criminal, have been preferred over them only because his talents were literary? Perhaps the answer, even by 1960 standards, was that no one should be executed. If this were not the answer, to give preference to Chessman over non-habitual criminals or even over nonliterary professional criminals seems unfair. Why should the State decide a man who can write has rehabilitated himself more than a man who truly decides that if he ever got the chance he would become the best ditch-digger in his county? Lodged deep down at the base of the whole argument is the fact that few others on death row managed to stay alive long enough to rehabilitate themselves. The fact Chessman did and that his talents happen to run to writing, the one type of self-expression possible on Death Row, should not have gained him preference over his fellow cellmates.

Except for fellow inmates, Louis S. Nelson knew Chessman better than anyone. For most of his last twelve years, Nelson was the Assistant Warden in charge of Death Row. Today Warden Nelson is the boss of San Quentin. Nelson's thirty-two years working at Alcatraz and San Quentin have brought most of this nation's worst criminals to his door. In an interview he named Chessman as the most arrogant criminal he ever encountered. He snorted at the idea that Chessman had rehabilitated himself and even dismissed the stories of his great intelligence:

> I never bought that genius tag. We have had plenty smarter fellows than him around here. Why Bob Lokey who is assigned to work in our prison fire engine company could run mental rings around Chessman. Lokey has invented and patented a Braille typewriter and a safety device for power saws. He is truly a bright fellow.

He ended our interview by reminding me that Chessman had said many nasty things about him in *The Face of Justice*. Thus he didn't mind having his own judgment put on paper. His parting words were: "No matter how times have changed, you just never could let that fellow back into society, no matter what."

Warden Nelson averred that any time the opportunity presented itself for Chessman to cause trouble, he did so. He claimed that it was Chessman who brought about a change in the Death Row recreation pattern. It had been the custom to open the cells one hour a day so the inmates could walk around. Well-patrolled as these periods were, Chessman managed to cause trouble, he said. Nelson was called at home one night because a Death Row prisoner was hysterical. After coming to the prison the Warden listened to the man ramble for fifteen minutes and pieced together a grizzly tale. During the recreation period that day, said the hysterical prisoner, a catlike Chessman pulled him into one of the open cells and secretly performed the identical action that Chessman had forced Regina Johnson and Mary Alice Meza to perform. Nelson put a lengthy account of this story in the San Quentin files (he and other wardens learned their lesson from Harley Teets' mistake in failing to leave a written record of the Barbara Graham confession incident), and from that day on only one cell remained open for toilet facilities during Death Row recreation hour at San Quentin.

Other than the hysterical prisoner, no witnesses exist as to this Death Row incident. Considering the source, the tale must be accepted as no more than probably true. Still, no motive is evident for the inmate to invent the story. Nelson could not get him off Death Row. Only the governor or a new trial could succeed. Why would the prisoner fake hysterics and lie? Assuming the tale is true, it adds to the evidence which can lead one to believe that Chessman committed the "red light" crimes and it raises doubts about his ability to live in close contact with a sizable portion of humanity, be it in prison or the outside world. If true, the act of Chessman was reckless in the extreme, whatever else it also may be. It would be another strike against him with the authorities. But, as many instances have demonstrated, Chessman was nothing if not reckless.

A counterweight to the kind of personality implied in Nelson's story of the prison attack is provided by longtime San Francisco crime reporter, Bernice Freeman Davis, in her book *The Desperate and the Damned*. One of Mrs. Davis' daughters was afflicted with bad eyesight. She recalled that Chessman started one of his interviews with her in the following manner:

> Look Bernie. I can fight all these bastards just as well with one eye as with two. If one of my eyes would do Patsy any good, I'd make arrangements at once. But, remember, not a word about this. If I see anything in the papers or a rumble that you have repeated it, it'll be a long time before you get another story .

Touching! Right? Still, does it sound like the Chessman we all know and love? The reason it doesn't ring true is contained elsewhere in the amiably chowderheaded account of Mrs. Davis. She also says that as a frequent visitor to San Quentin, many of the convicts knew her daughter's eye trouble was irremediable and a transplant would do no good. She underrates the pervasiveness of prison gossip. The grapevine easily can climb over the wall into Death Row. Chessman's offer was a safe bet.

Another witness, Clinton Duffy, takes the same view as Nelson concerning Chessman. Duffy was warden at San Quentin when Chessman arrived in 1948. Although he was a prison official, he opposed capital punishment, but he refused to see Chessman as an ally in that cause. The following sober account is taken from *88 Men and 2 Women* by Duffy and professional writer, Al Hirschberg. The title refers to the number of people executed at San Quentin while Duffy was in charge of the prison:

> I knew Caryl Chessman well, and if he is ever recognized as a martyr, it will be a travesty. Chessman was one of the most dangerous men I ever knew, for he combined the brains of a savant with the morals of a degenerate, the polish of a gentleman with the heart of a scamp. He charmed almost every outsider he met during his twelve years on death row, but he hated them all, for they represented "society" which meant decency and law and order and authority. It is my belief that Chessman considered "society" his natural enemy and he clung to his resentment of all phases of it to the day of his death.
>
> His ability to make a lasting impression on the people who sat across from him in the condemned men's visiting room was fantastic, particularly since he never tried to hide his resentment.

On the contrary, he exploited it. I know of no other convict who dared to do this, for resentment makes enemies and leads to trouble. When any other prisoner got into a jam, his friends outside asked, "Why can't Joe behave?" When Chessman got into one, his friends outside asked, "How can you blame him after what he's been through?"

At his worst Caryl Chessman was very bad indeed. In death row he was a tough prisoner to handle—mean, demanding, contemptuous, arrogant and defiant. Nearly always in the middle or the cause of an argument, he made life so miserable for the guards that they almost welcomed a chance to lock him up for a few days. Chessman treated them like lackeys. He insisted on his "rights" and threatened everyone with "exposure" if he didn't get what he wanted when he wanted it. He took every favor as a matter of course, and then asked for more. I never heard him say "thanks" as if he meant it. There was always a smirk on his face, as if he were ashamed of showing his appreciation.

He was the worst griper in the row's history. He objected to noises in the isolation cell block next door to the row; and, when it was quiet there, demanded that the men in the main yard six floors below talk in whispers so he could do his work. He insisted on bonded paper of exact dimensions for his endless writs and pleas and petitions, and he always found something wrong with his typewriter. He pounced on every excuse to make a demand, for demands harassed the guards and harassing guards was one of the few things that gave Chessman pleasure.

Chessman got into innumerable fights on death row. One day he and Louis F. Smith, a fellow prisoner, had an argument over the proper wording of a writ that Chessman was writing. Within minutes they were flailing away at each other. Before the officers could break it up, Chessman put a pencil through Smith's cheek. Chessman once organized a hunger strike on the row. Another time he started a free-for-all fight because the Christmas tree wasn't big enough to suit him. He and several others refused to return to their cells after the recreation one day and it took half-a-dozen husky guards to put them where they belonged.

Chessman may yet become a martyr to the cause of the abolition of capital punishment. I hope he never does for he was not the martyr type. An ex-con who knew him well told me recently, "Caryl Chessman had brains but no wisdom." I never heard a better description of the man.

In his book, *Behind Bars*, about his days as San Quentin chaplain, Rabbi Julius A. Leibert includes a most revealing short comment by Eddie Wein: "You know why I think Chessman fights so hard for his life? He wants another chance to shoot it out with the cops. He'd rather die with a gun in his hand than like a cockroach."

As suggested earlier, arguments for commutation which rest on the idea of repentance or rehabilitation are really pretty nebulous. Prison is such a controlled atmosphere, lacking any resemblance to conditions in the outside world, that it is hard to say whether or how a man has changed. This problem is compounded when it is said that clemency should be granted because a man has had a religious conversion. But in at least two cases, religious piety was the operative if not specifically stated ground for commutations by Pat Brown. First of all, "want-ad rapist" Eddie Wein, sentenced to death under Sec. 209, was spared at the insistence of Rabbi Leibert, San Quentin's Jewish chaplain who resigned to win public support for his campaign to have Wein's sentence commuted. In a similar case, George T. Davis won clemency for a convicted murderer, son of a Greek Orthodox priest. "I had so many bearded priests with black robes in the governor's office," recalls Davis, "I bet it took Pat a month to get rid of the incense smell!"

Given his past track record, it is surprising that Chessman didn't claim that he had experienced a religious conversion. He tried everything else. However, a religious conversion would have necessitated making room for God in his ego. When dwelling on his wonderful capacities, Chessman didn't want any visitors. Maybe it was pride rather than honesty that kept Chessman from claiming conversion. Whether true or not, certain authorities claim in all seriousness that Chessman constantly hoped that the Friday of his execution, the traditional day for executions, would be Good Friday.

A second ground which Governor Brown could have used to grant Chessman clemency was the length of his stay on Death Row. The reasons for doing so are well explained in a letter sent to the Governor by William Bennett, then Deputy Attorney General of California, in February 1960. At that point, Chessman was scheduled to be executed on February 19. Because of its good sense this long letter from one of the Government attorneys in the case will be quoted in its entirety. It should be noted that at that time it was a courageous act for any public official to take a stand in favor of leniency for Chessman.

February 16, 1960

The Honorable Edmund G. Brown
Governor of California
Executive Offices
State Capitol
Sacramento, California

Subject: In Re Caryl Chessman
Dear Pat:

In furtherance of our conversation in your office concerning the Chessman case, I am writing to you to express my views upon any executive action which is permitted to you at this point in the case.

As you know, I have a familiarity with the past legal proceedings concerning Caryl Chessman. I was first assigned to this matter by you in the latter part of 1955 to represent the State of California in the hearing held in the Federal District Court in San Francisco before the Honorable Louis E. Goodman. This was a hearing which had been directed by the United States Supreme Court, for the purpose of inquiring into certain claims which had been made by Chessman. These proceedings extended three weeks, and in order to represent the State of California it was necessary that I make myself familiar with all aspects of the prior proceedings pertaining to Caryl Chessman. After the proceedings had terminated before Judge Goodman, I thereafter argued the Chessman case on behalf of the State of California before the United States Supreme Court in the October Term, 1956.

I point out to you my association with this case so as to make it clear to you that I am quite familiar with the record herein and with all of the claims advanced from time to time by Caryl Chessman.

I long ago concluded that all of the various claims advanced by Chessman are without merit. Never at any time nor now have I entertained the slightest doubt as to his guilt.

This portion of the proceedings involving Caryl Chessman is, however, now concluded. The question before you now is whether or not you should exercise the power granted you by Article VII of the California Constitution, whereby you are permitted to grant a commutation of sentence, if proper. It is my judgment, for reasons which I shall state hereafter, that Caryl Chessman's sentence of death should be commuted to life imprisonment.

Comments have been made concerning the arrogance of Caryl Chessman, his pose of superiority, and, above all his failure to apply to you for relief. I do not agree with those who take a narrow construction of this case and use any of these things as a basis upon which you can deny relief if you once decide that execution after almost twelve years is not proper. Regardless of the qualities of character which Chessman is said to possess, and regardless of his failure to seek relief from you, it is my opinion that, being familiar with the case as you are, and having an awareness of the long delay between the trial date herein and a possible execution date, you are confronted squarely with the question, as Governor, of whether or not the long delay in this case is sufficient reason for you to invoke your constitutional power and to commute the death sentence of Caryl Chessman. It is my opinion, and I certainly have no claim to infallibility here, that it would be a proper act of mercy upon your part to grant commutation to Caryl Chessman.

I realize that people of opposite opinions, equally motivated by persuasive reasons and good faith are convinced that the sentence should be carried out here. My objection to execution in this case comes from the unreasonable delay which has marked the case from the beginning. I realize very well that Caryl Chessman himself has been the prime factor in causing delay. Despite this, however, the judicial system has seen fit to permit delay here and, whether caused by Chessman or properly permitted by the courts, the inescapable fact is that almost twelve years have elapsed from the date sentence was pronounced to the execution date, now set for February 19. I want to emphasize that there is no criticism here of the courts, since due process, as lawyers know, has a way of taking more time than expected.

The basis of my recommendation lies in the inordinate delay attendant upon this case. If the execution in this matter had followed within a reasonable period from the date sentence was pronounced, the matter, of course, would long since have been disposed of and the problem would not be before you today. The delay, however, is a factor which cannot be ignored, even though Caryl Chessman has been the most causative factor thereto.

In view of the years which have intervened from the time sentence was pronounced, I am of the personal opinion that justice would not be served by taking the life of this man. This case reflects now upon our system of government as it dispenses justice. The justice here was neither certain nor sure, and it is somewhat anticlimactic after twelve years now to invoke the death penalty, even admitting the fact that Caryl Chessman himself has caused the very delay by which he benefits.

You, as a lawyer, know that it is most difficult to spell out in concise terms the meaning which due process has acquired in the courts. So, also, it is likewise difficult to spell out those things which prompt one to recommend that you extend mercy to Caryl Chessman. The arguments on both sides of the question are seemingly endless, and if this letter be prompted by no more than my notions of justice and respect for human life, I can only conclude by saying that I recommend to you that commutation be here granted.

Best personal regards,

s/William M. Bennett

Though it may be surprising, Chessman's twelve year stay on Death Row was not as far over the average as one might think. (See charts 3 and 4.) Why such a consistent pattern of delay? The answer is found in Section 1239(b) of the California Penal Code: "When upon any plea a judgement of death is rendered, an appeal is automatically taken by the defendant without any action by him or his counsel." This appeal is not a hit-or-miss thing. The California Supreme Court carefully reviews the trial transcript to see if error necessitating reversal occurred. An excellent study in the *Stanford Law Review* discloses that between 1942 and 1956, ten months was the average amount of time consumed from date of death sentence to the date of the California Supreme Court Decision on the appeal. Nineteen percent of this time was consumed in the preparation of the

CHART 3   Months from Admission with Death Sentence to Execution (California felons executed) [a]

Months on Death Row	1950-1954			1955-1959			1960-1964		
	Number Executed	Percent	Cumulative Percent	Number Executed	Percent	Cumulative Percent	Number Executed	Percent	Cumulative Percent
8-12	22	56.4	56.4	9	25.7	25.7	5	17.3	17.3
13-18	9	23.1	79.5	5	14.3	40.0	16	55.2	72.5
19-24	2	5.1	84.6	10 [b]	28.6	68.6	1	3.4	75.9
25-36	3	7.7	92.3	2	5.7	74.3	2	6.9	82.8
37-48	2	5.1	97.4	2	5.7	80.0	4 [c]	13.8	96.6
49 and over	1	2.6	100.0	7	20.0	100.0	1	3.4	100.0
Total	39	100.0		35	100.0		29	100.0	

[a] During 1965-1970, only one man was executed. He was sentenced for murder in the first degree and was executed April 12, 1967 after thirty months on death row.
[b] Figure includes one woman, Barbara Graham, executed for first degree murder on June 3, 1955.
[c] Figure includes one woman, Elizabeth Ann Duncan, executed for first degree murder on September 8, 1962.

CHART 4 **Months Spent on Death Row and Ultimate Disposition of Persons Sentenced to Death in California (1942-1956)**

Months on Death Row	Executed	Reversed	Modified	Commuted	Suicide	Remaining on Row as of 1/1/57	Miscellaneous
0-3	3	2	—	—	2	—	—
4-6	12	7	1	—	1	—	2[a]
7-9	34	9	1	1	—	—	—
10-12	30	6	2	1	2	—	—
13-16	15	1	1	2	—	—	—
17-20	9	—	—	—	1	—	2[b]
21-24	5	—	—	5	—	2	1[c]
25-36	3	—	—	1	—	2	—
37-60	5	—	—	—	—	1	—
61-72	1	—	—	1	—	1	—
73-84	2	—	—	—	—	1	—
84	—	—	—	—	—	—	—
Total	119	25	6	11	6	8	5

[a] One man died of natural causes; one died trying to escape.
[b] New trial on *coram nobis*.
[c] Declared insane prior to execution date.

record, 45 percent in filing briefs and hearing arguments, 36 percent in deliberation of the court. These figures were found to be nearly identical with similar statistics for the period from 1929 to 1935. The average wait in the fifty-eight automatic appeals considered during that period was also ten months; 18 percent in preparation of the record, 50 percent in filing briefs and hearing arguments, and 32 percent in deliberation of the court.

Therefore Chessman and all others sentenced to death had a substantial breather while the automatic appeal was being considered. Once the Supreme Court has made a decision on the automatic appeal, unfavorable to the condemned man, it is up to him as to whether further legal action is taken. During the fifteen-year period studied by the *Stanford Law Review,* 145 of the 180 automatic appeals were denied: sixty-two of those prisoners who had their appeals denied, took no further action; fifty-five of them were ultimately executed (355 days was the average length of this group's stay on Death Row). The remaining eighty-three, all together, filed postconviction petitions in state or federal court. As of 1956, the end of the period considered in the Stanford study, only sixty-four had been executed (761 days was the average length of this group's stay on Death Row). One actually obtained his release from prison.

The point is not that those who kept fighting were more successful than those who gave up after losing the automatic appeal. Remember, the survey stopped as of January 1, 1957; after that date, some of those still in the process of battling the grim reaper, lost. Chessman is one of those. In all, the percentage of those who were executed is roughly the same for the further petitioners and the nonfurther petitioners. What is not the same is the length of their stay on Death Row. Each additional avenue of escape that was explored took time. As with the automatic appeal, time must be extended in each supplementary appeal for preparation of the record, the filing of briefs, hearing of arguments and deliberating upon a decision. This is especially true when it is a federal court rather than a California state court considering the matter, because usually the state court has already considered the matter and so is familiar with prior proceedings in the case.

A condemned man cannot go on appealing endlessly. Eventually appellate courts will say they have already considered the matter and refuse to hear the new appeal. When this happens, the jig is up. Traditionally courts have been slow to blow the whistle in capital cases. No judge likes to feel that he has the final responsibility for an execution, no matter how just the decision. Chessman capitalized on this. He kept knocking on all doors looking for someone to listen to his latest plea. Each time he found a receptive ear, the clock stopped running for a while. But there are only so many doors. After a while, Chessman returned, three or four times, to the same doors—always with the same basic argument: No transcript existed and thus the California Supreme Court could not rule legitimately on his automatic appeal.

It was in 1957, on his fourth sortie on the transcript question, that the United States Supreme Court bought his argument and ordered the California courts to hold a full hearing on the matter. It was at this point that Justice William O. Douglas blew his stack and in his dissent charged, in a fuller version of a quote given at the beginning of this book: "The conclusion is irresistible that Chessman is playing a game with the courts, stalling for time while the facts grow cold." Mr. Justice Felix Frankfurter, writing for the majority, answered Douglas with the testy comment:

> Evidently, it also needs to be repeated that the overriding responsibility of this Court is to the Constitution of the United States, no matter how late it may be that a violation of the Constitution is found to exist. This Court may not disregard the Constitution because an appeal in this case, as in others, has been made on the eve of execution. We must be deaf to all suggestions that a valid appeal to the Constitution even by a guilty man, comes too late because courts, including this Court, were not earlier able to enforce what the Constitution demands. The proponent before the Court is not the petitioner but the Constitution of the United States.

Despite the logic of the majority's position, Douglas was not totally out of bounds in his criticism. This was the seventh time Chessman had taken his case to the United States Supreme

Court, the fourth time on this specific point of law. Until 1957, no justice had voted to remand the case for further hearings. Why did a majority of the Justices suddenly change their minds? It is strictly Monday-morning quarterbacking to speculate on the reasons this long after the fact. However, anyone reading the transcript of the November 1955 *habeas corpus* hearing before Judge Louis E. Goodman is entitled to a guess. In the early part of this hearing, some of the statements of His Honor were so intemperate as to raise serious question of his impartiality. Make no mistake: facts existed for Goodman to rule against Chessman. It is not that he was wrong. However, some of the Justices may have been reluctant to bring down the curtain on Chessman with such a discordant third act. Very probably, the Court didn't really believe the transcript was inadequate, but felt this should be demonstrated in an orderly court. The full hearing they ordered was magnificently chaired by Judge Walter R. Evans. Like Goodman, Evans found against Chessman. The manner in which he did helped mightily to clear the air.

The appeal process is one of the most unsatisfactory parts of the American criminal justice system. Delay, confusion, duplication, and error mark each appeal to some extent. In Chessman's case, all these disadvantages were maximized. It is beyond the scope of this book to examine in detail the appeals. Which court had authority to hear which appeal and under what circumstances is most complicated. For those interested in this subject, a well-written study which appeared in 1961 in the *Minnesota Law Review* should be the starting point for inquiry.

No question—twelve years on Death Row is a dreadful way to go out: never breathing fresh air, counting the days, locked in a cell twenty-three hours a day, watching ninety-two companions leave by the gas-chamber door. But it must be remembered that Chessman was not on Death Row that much longer than many others and at all times the courts were considering his appeals. He did no more than exercise his rights to appeal more effectively than others. His opponents acted as if he should shut up and be gassed. This speaks poorly of their appreciation of our legal system. Their proper concern should have been that all legitimate questions were timely heard, and decided; and then, justice, whatever it dictates, be accomplished. It is ironic that the same men who sat in front of the television on Saturday afternoons applauding college quarterbacks scrambling to evade large linemen, would hurl invectives at Caryl Chessman scrambling to stay alive. Consistency is not always an American strong point.

Twelve years on Death Row may be reason for a governor to grant clemency, but it is not "cruel and unusual." Chessman should not be blamed. If the laws concerning appeals are poorly drawn and sloppily applied, change the laws; don't censure the man who uses the law as written. The delay highlights both the solicitude and inefficiency of American law. It also brought out the unwillingness of many citizens to abide by the spirit of American law when the results are not to their pleasing.

Most of those howling for Chessman's scalp really didn't know what he was convicted for. A scholarly article on "Federal Control of State Criminal Justice," published in 1957 in the *Missouri Law Review,* contained the following remarkable statement: "Of the other cases of this variety, the one which has attracted the most publicity and attention is that of Caryl Chessman, convicted rapist-murderer in California." Reading something like this in a prestigious journal is both depressing and frustrating. That the author, Richard C. Baker, had the best possible professional credentials—A.B., Harvard College; A.M., Cornell University; Ph.D., Columbia University; Member New York Bar—only heightens the frustration. Baker and the assisting members of the *Missouri Law Review* who, today, undoubtedly are leading lawyers and judges of that state, deserve the harshest condemnation. Chessman was *not* a murderer; to name him as one and then to go on to criticize his constant use of the appellate process is the best possible illustration why courts permitted extensive review of this case.

Alexander Gregg of the Rockefeller Foundation provides a good explanation for the many misconceptions that sprang up in the Chessman case. In the forward to the Kinsey Report, *Sexual Behavior in the Human Male,* published in 1948, he wrote:

> As long as sex is dealt with in the current confusion of ignorance and sophistication, denial and indulgence, suppression and

stimulation, punishment and exploitation, secrecy and display, it will be associated with a duplicity and indecency that lead neither to intellectual honesty nor human dignity.

Kinsey and his associates reiterate this point when discussing their findings concerning the activity in which Chessman engaged:

> Before marriage, the percentages of males with histories which included mouth stimulation of the male genitalia during hetero-sexual relations were 22, 30 and 39% of educational levels 0-8, 9-12, 13 +; respectively. After marriage, 7, 15 and 43% respectively.
> . . . Because of the longstanding taboos in our culture on mouth genital activity, it is quite probable that there has been more cover-up on this point than on most others in the present study, and the above figures must, therefore, represent minimal incidences.

The Kinsey Report was talking about voluntary activity, not involuntary as in the Chessman case. Yet the crimes committed by Chessman became buried in the general taboos on this subject mentioned by the Kinsey Report. The crimes were termed "unspeakable." As often happens, this leads to exaggeration. Many people thought he was a murderer; others thought he was a combination of the Boston Strangler and Jack the Ripper. All sorts of wild claims were made. The myth replaced the reality.

In 1955, the California Legislature passed a joint resolution demanding that Congress investigate laws relating to repeated use of *habeas corpus* by prisoners convicted in state courts. In the petition, Chessman was named as the best example of a state prisoner abusing the procedure. That a legislature composed mostly of lawyers would pass a resolution of this type referring directly to a case still in the appellate process is a sad commentary on their observation of the spirit of American law. Even more interesting is the group of epitaphs used to describe Chessman (keep in mind, this an official action of the Legislature of the State of California). Chessman is described as "a convicted sex terrorist and kidnapper;" "an infamous criminal;" "a depraved person;" "a brutal and fiendish sex pervert;" and "a depraved sex terrorist." How many legislators who voted for these resolutions had an accurate idea of the crimes which Chessman had commited? Probably few.

In 1968 a Swedish husband and wife writing team, Maj Sjowal and Per Wahloo, published an excellent mystery, *Roseanna*. Their hero, Stockholm police detective, Martin Beck, sought the sex killer responsible for eliminating the girl named in the title. At one point, Beck gave himself a few words of good advice. It is too bad that he was not around Sacramento in 1955, because some members of the California Legislature could have profited from the following:

> "Remember that you have three of the most important virtues a policeman can have," he thought. "You are stubborn and logical, and completely calm. You don't allow yourself to lose your composure and you act only professionally on a case, whatever it is. Words like repulsive, horrible and bestial belong in the newspapers, not in your thinking. A murderer is a regular human being, only more unfortunate and maladjusted."

Some of the factual misstatements in the Chessman case would be laughable if a man's life were not involved. Not all these fables were unfavorable to Chessman. We have pointed out instances in which Chessman forces created their own myths. Such myth-making, as shown earlier, was a central feature of Chessman's own works, and also of the book by Machlin and Woodfield. But, if possible, it was even more frequent in the books written on Chessman by foreigners. They were largely fairy tales. The number of errors are too great to recount. One brief example is the way that Julio Camerero, a Spanish reporter, claimed in some colorful passages that along with Chessman were executed Elizabeth Ann Duncan and two male accomplices, three people condemned in a murder case, who were, in fact, executed only in September 1962. But the myths and misstatements of the pro-Chessman forces did not mislead the public and the authorities and take a man's life.

In fact, Governor Brown could have granted clemency on the theory that people wanted Chessman executed for crimes he did not commit. In urging the death penalty, the *Los Angeles Times*, in a February 1960 editorial, stated that Chessman had committed "indescribable crimes whose horrible details are hidden in the decent exclusiveness of court records." It is precisely because the details were obscured and exaggerated that Brown could have granted clemency. Instead, he denied clemency on the basis of the questionable claim that Chessman had driven Mary Alice Meza into insanity.

Everyone who spoke out on the Chessman case in demonstrable ignorance of the crimes he had committed deserves censure. It appears Chessman was executed more for the crimes that respectable people manufactured in their sordid imaginations than for the crimes that he actually committed. The bitter statement by Chessman that the devil would have to work hard to match the tortures perpetrated by the State of California is not totally without basis in fact.

The bars Caryl Chessman used to haunt on Hollywood Boulevard are no longer there. Today, the space is employed to sell pornographic books and show sex films twenty-four hours a day. It is more lucrative than selling whiskey. Drugged college students and bewildered child runaways clog this famous street. The glamour is gone; only glitter and tinsel remain.

What about the central actors in the Chessman case? Chessman is dead, of course. But who remains and how do they feel when their statements in the case are recalled?

J. Miller Leavy is still in residence at the Los Angeles Hall of Justice. Today he is Director of Operations for the gigantic office of the Los Angeles District Attorney, overseeing 450 prosecutors. Completing his fortieth year on the job, Leavy is acknowledged by all as one of the most skillful trial lawyers ever to work for Los Angeles County. Say what one will about Leavy, and a lot of people object to his Death-Valley-Days style of prosecution, he makes no effort to hide his role in the Chessman affair and is ready to explain and defend all his actions in that case. This cannot be said about everyone involved.

The people who have tried to change their public image most are former Governor Pat Brown and his Clemency Secretary, Cecil Poole. The name Edmund G. Brown can be found on the list of those filing *amicus curiae* briefs against the death penalty in the 1972 Furman case. This should not be a surprise; Brown always was an outspoken foe of capital punishment when that was convenient. On May 2, 1960, it was not convenient. This kind of shift on issues is not at all untypical of Brown. When he was governor, he vowed undying opposition to the idea of El Paso Natural Gas Company developing a pipeline in California, a pipeline which would give the company a monopoly of natural gas in the state. On this issue he made the kind of forceful stand people had hoped he would make in the Chessman case. Today he has flip-flopped and is an outspoken advocate of the El Paso pipeline.

Clemency Secretary Poole is now an open proponent for the abolition of the death penalty. He eventually became the chairperson of the American Bar Association's 35,000-member Individual Rights and Responsibilities Section. Given the harshness of his statements against Chessman, and his well-known, long-time refusal to enter into discussion of the matter, his present-day flowery statements about the inalienable rights of all Americans make interesting reading.

William Bennett is still battling Pat Brown, today over the issue of the El Paso natural gas monopoly. Bennett is now Chairman of the California Board of Equalization, the State taxing authority and has achieved fame speaking out for the little man when he thinks he deserves a better deal. He also has challenged former President Nixon on tax questions concerning the San Clemente "White House." Bennett never thought Chessman was right, but he did think he deserved a better deal than execution. Bennett displays proudly to all visitors the note of congratulation he received from Mr. Justice Frankfurter for skill in argument before the United States Supreme Court in the Chessman case. Frankfurter handed out two such notes in his long career. When Bennett spoke out on a subject, he spoke out well. Today, he is a firm opponent of capital punishment. He realizes that every capital case stands the chance of becoming a circus, like the Chessman case. He knows the bad effect circuses have on American justice and doesn't want to see any more of them.

The two lawyers most involved in the defense of the Chessman case still are on the scene. George T. Davis is as successful as ever. Today his practice runs more to complicated income tax evasion cases than to crimes of violence. He hasn't lost his love of seeing his name in the paper. At the same time his skills as an attorney are acknowledged by all, friend and foe. Davis gave Chessman his money's worth in defense. Chessman gave Davis more ammunition in his life-long ideological fight against the death penalty. It was a fair trade.

Rosalie Asher is no longer engaged in the active practice of the law. Her health broke down shortly after the Chessman case. During her long years of giving legal assistance to Chessman, she had become his friend. She is executrix of the estate and the only principal in the case convinced of his innocence. A dozen years after the end of the Chessman affair, the opposing lawyers still do not have the kindest words to say about each other. The only exception is when discussing Miss Asher. All agree that she acted at all times with utmost courtesy and with total devotion to the cause of her client.

This book ends without any startling claims of innocence for Chessman—no charges that he was not properly convicted, or even, given the cultural mores of 1948, that he should not have been sentenced to death (as opposed to being executed). What it does conclude is that from the start to finish all those involved lost their sense of balance. Everyone chose up sides, and, instead of reasoning each step out independently, let their roles dictate what they should do next. If this case occurred today, I fear everyone would still choose sides and allow mindless rhetoric to dictate what would happen.

A. J. McAloon in a review of *Cell 2455, Death Row*, in the June 19, 1954 issue of *America,* raised the really fundamental question of the Chessman case: "This reviewer believes that due to his background, he never would have been able to function normally. But, should we execute abnormals?" Today we wouldn't execute Chessman, merely lock him in San Quentin and throw away the key. Somehow, it doesn't seem like much of a solution.

part 2

The Trial Transcript

When Caryl Chessman's case came to the California Supreme Court on automatic appeal after his death penalty sentence conviction, the first problem the court faced concerned the trial transcript. A quick summary should bring the facts to mind. The court reporter during the trial, Ernest R. Perry, died shortly after the trial when about one-third of the trial testimony had yet to be transcribed. Judge Fricke denied Chessman's sentencing-day motion for a new trial on the basis of an inadequate record because of the reporter's death, and left the transcript question to the decision of the California Supreme Court. Then, at the suggestion of Prosecutor Leavy, he set about to hire someone else to read and transcribe Perry's notes. The man he chose was Stanley Fraser, a court reporter who had known Perry. Later, during the bitterly contested court battle over the transcript, it came out that Fraser was both an alcoholic and a relation, although a distant one (an uncle by marriage), of Prosecutor J. Miller Leavy. Leavy admitted he had mentioned the name of Fraser to Fricke.

It is widely held that an accurate trial transcript is essential for a fair trial. Thus, many say that when the court reporter dies before the transcript of the evidence is properly prepared, a new trial should be granted. This is the view, for instance, of the respected legal authority, Lester Orfield, author of *Criminal Procedure From Arrest to Appeal.* On the other hand, it is possible to cite, as the California Supreme Court did, the 1908 California case, *State* v. *Botkin*, which says; "It is incumbent on the appellant to show error, and we know of no rule that permits us to presume that the defendant did not have a fair trial because a portion of the record upon . . . appeal has been destroyed without fault of either party."

The United States Supreme Court has permitted this line of reasoning. In a 1972 case, *Meyer* v. *Chicago*, it reaffirmed a holding made earlier in *Draper* v. *Chicago*: "Alternate methods of reporting trial proceedings are permissible if they place before the appellate court an equivalent report of the events at trial from which the appellant's contentions arise."

Chessman remained alive for twelve years while contesting whether the alternate method was adequate. Did the attempt of Fraser to read and transcribe Perry's shorthand notes provide the appellate court with an equivalent report of the events at trial from which the appellant's contentions arose? The legal crux of all his appeals can be stated this concisely. The form of his appeal was a habeas corpus petition claiming that he was being improperly held in jail. His petition went again and again to the California and United States Supreme Courts.

The courts gave Chessman no breaks on the point. In effect, they sat back and said, "Sure the transcript is adequate. If you say it isn't, prove it. Even if you can prove it, then show us that the omissions are sufficiently prejudicial to you to demand an overturning of the guilty verdict." A heavy burden. In general, the courts appeared more interested in upholding the principle that a trial is presumed regular until proven otherwise than in the principle that the state will not execute anyone unless there be total compliance with constitutional guarantees.

Finally, a court-ordered hearing on the transcript was held before Judge Walter R. Evans in late 1957 and early 1958. In that proceeding, as earlier, Chessman never could point conclusively to specific matter occurring in the trial that was unrecorded by

Perry or materially mistranscribed by Fraser, let alone show the omissions or errors were gravely prejudicial. But he fought hard. The hearing virtually turned into a battle over how Fraser had transcribed each of Perry's symbols. It lasted fifty-five days and the record of it fills 6,000 single-spaced pages. From this mass, a brief selection of highlights will be presented. For the most part, the material speaks for itself. As he had done nine years before at his 1948 trial, Chessman ran his whole show. Again a mistake, especially because by 1957 he had sold enough books to hire any attorney he wished. Although shrewd and probing questions were often posed, he never had a specific game plan. In the long run he would have benefitted if one of the competent lawyers assisting him had presented the case. If this had happened, it is likely his main points would not have become lost in a mound of triviality.

Once Chessman lost this 1957 transcript hearing, it was all down hill to the gas chamber. The highpoint of his massive legal resistance had been reached. He had no more ammunition, althoughthe case dragged on for two more years. The crucial date of the beginning of the end for Chessman was February 28, 1958. This was the day that Judge Evans made 2,000 corrections in the Perry-Fraser transcript and then certified it as being sufficiently accurate for the California State Supreme Court to use it as a basis for ruling on the automatic appeal granted to all condemned prisoners by Section 1239(b) of the State Penal Code. It goes almost without saying that Chessman, again, lost this automatic appeal. He also lost his challenges against some ninety of the corrections Judge Evans had made in the transcript.

Before proceeding to the hearing testimony, I would like to clear up a few matters. Over the years, the claim that 105 pages of the trial transcript were lost has become one of the legends associated with this case. As can be expected, Chessman was the instigator of this claim. Ernest Perry had transcribed 593 typewritten pages from fifteen hours and forty-five minutes of trial testimony before death halted his work. From this Chessman calculated that Perry had transcribed 379 pages from each trial hour. Fraser completed the transcribing of the remaining thirty-four hours and twenty minutes of trial testimony in 1,194 typewritten pages. This averages, by Chessman's calculation, to 348 pages per trial hour. From this, Chessman made the questionable deduction Fraser had failed to transcribe 3.1 pages per hour of Perry's symbols. For thirty-four hours, this meant he missed 105 pages. *Voila!* The 105 missing pages.

The missing-pages argument of Chessman does not impress crack New York Supreme Court courtroom reporter, Tom Cole. "It ignores too many variables," points out Cole. "Speed in speaking. Time used to reflect before answering. Quick conferences between attorney and client. The number of times two people talk at the same time. No two hours would ever be the same. I'd be worried if there weren't a 5 percent to 10 percent variance," Cole observed. "In fact, I could see a variance up to 20 percent without any real hint of irregularity occurring. The 9 percent variation in the Chessman case is a normal amount."

Some readers might wonder whether the judge at the trial, Judge Fricke, could have granted Chessman a new trial on his own motion and, thus, cut off any possible trouble before it started. The answer is no. Section 1181 of the California Penal Code provides seven grounds for a judge in a criminal case to grant a new trial on his own motion: (1) absence of defendant from the trial; (2) receiving of evidence out of court by the jury; (3) misconduct of the jury; (4) deciding of verdict by lot; (5) error in instruction of law to jury and prejudicial misconduct by the prosecuting attorney; (6) verdict being contrary to law or evidence; (7) new evidence discovered after trial. Death of courtroom reporter before transcription is completed is conspicuously absent. Thus the trial judge was powerless to grant a new trial for this reason. Had he done so, he would have been requiring that the defendant be tried twice for the same crime. This is not permitted. If Fricke had granted Chessman a new trial, *sua sponte*, because of the death of Perry, in actuality he would have given Chessman his freedom. Jeopardy would attach and Chessman never could be tried again on the same charges.

Surprisingly, if it had been a civil case, Fricke, if so disposed, could have acted on his own under the authority of California Code of Civil Procedure Section 953(e):

When it shall be impossible to have a stenographic record of the trial transcribed by a stenographic reporter as provided by law or rule, because of the death or disability of a reporter who participated as a stenographic reporter at the trial, or because of the loss or destruction, in whole or in substantial part, of the notes of such reporter, the court or a judge thereof shall have power to set aside and vacate the judgment, order or decree from which an appeal has been taken or is to be taken and to order a new trial of the action or proceeding.

Why such a common-sense rule was not also passed to cover criminal trials is a mystery. Still, the power to order a new trial for this reason in a civil case was discretionary with the judge. Fricke probably would have refused even if possessing the power.

If the Chessman trial occurred today, a similar transcript dispute could happen again if no daily transcript was kept. If the reporter still wrote his notes with pen and ink, the situation would be identical. Of course far fewer reporters today handwrite their courtroom notes than in 1948. The machine has made great inroads. It is physically far less demanding to tap a keyboard than to be a scrivener. This is not necessarily an improvement in the quality of courtroom reporting. Certainly, difficulty in reading penmanship is eliminated by using the machine. This gain is compensated for by a loss in accuracy. Since it is easier to tap than to write, the attention of reporters can wander and mistakes of carelessness occur more often than when a man is writing with pen and ink. On the whole, it is about a toss-up between machine and handwritten shorthand. If Chessman were faced with a present-day reporter who used the machine, he would have to limit his claims to the fact that the reporter missed a lot of testimony. There would be no problem reading it.

Somehow or other, we can guess that the combative Chessman would still cause confusion if the reporter died before completing transcription of his notes. Times haven't changed that much in the last quarter of a century. Chessman, himself, was an accomplished stenographer and typist. He was self-taught and had done secretarial work for prison officials at Folsom, Chino and San Quentin. He knew full well that some of his claims concerning the stenography in the case were ridiculous. However, that never stopped him from making untrue charges. His charges would be different today, but the intent identical. Confusion, not truth, was his motto.

What about tape recorders? To laymen, they would seem to answer all difficulties. Professionals say to the contrary. The State of Alaska adopted a system replacing live stenographers with tape recorders. Cost has far exceeded success: witnesses mumble or speak inaudibly; background noises intrude; malfunctions occur in the recording system; tapes are unintentionally erased or left on playback rather than record. The errors preclude general acceptance. Courtroom reporters remain a vital necessity. It is a highly skilled, demanding profession. Precisely because of the difficulty of their task, it is easy to make groundless claims that their work was deficient. They always will be hard pressed to prove it wasn't. When a full investigation is made of the work of the courtroom reporters in two famous California cases, *Chessman* and *Robillard*, the product in each case stands up well under close scrutiny.

Old-timers around the Los Angeles courts remember an amusing kind of incident which occurred often during the Chessman trial transcript hearing. It was a cold, rainy winter in Los Angeles. Each day, the two prosecutors, Leavy and Clifford Crail, also a Deputy District Attorney, had to trudge from their office to the courtroom fifteen minutes away. Frequently a large well-heated County Sheriff's Office car passed them on their way. It was detailed to transport Chessman from the jail to the courtroom. Appreciating the humor of the situation, the snugly warm Chessman would wave out the window to his opponents.

Our study of the 1957 transcript hearing will be divided into eight sections: (1) The Hiring of Stanley Fraser; (2) The Drinking of Stanley Fraser; (3) The Family Relationship Between Fraser and Leavy; (4) Possible Collusion with Prosecution and Police; (5) The Quality of the Perry Notes; (6) The Quality of the Fraser Transcription; (7) The Text of the Decision of Judge Evans; and (8) Concluding Observations.

The Hiring of Stanley Fraser

CRAIL:[1] Mr. Fraser, how old are you?

FRASER: Sixty-three.

CRAIL: And where were you born?

FRASER: South Dakota.

CRAIL: During the past thirty-five years, what has been your business or occupation?

FRASER: Court reporter.

CRAIL: And have you been one of the official reporters of this court?[2]

FRASER: Yes, sir.

CRAIL: When did that employment begin?

FRASER: I worked in the Superior Court in 1926, but I was not appointed as an official until 1927, I think sometime in October.

CRAIL: So that you worked continuously, by temporary or permanent appointment, from sometime in 1926 until what date?

FRASER: As I remember, it was along in the middle of the summer, 1953.

CRAIL: During that time, you were occupied, daily, with your duties as a court official, court reporter; is that correct?

FRASER: Yes.

CRAIL: Did you know Ernest R. Perry in his lifetime?

FRASER: I did.

CRAIL: When did you first meet Mr. Perry?

FRASER: Oh, I think it was in the spring of 1914.

CRAIL: And where did you meet him at that time?

FRASER: Seattle, Washington.

CRAIL: What was your association with him at that time?

FRASER: We were both working as official reporters in the Superior Court of the State of Washington, in and for King County, at Seattle. . . . It was a friendly association of two people engaged in the same occupation and working out of the same office. We would go to the court up on the hill in Seattle, in the old court house up there and come back down in the evening and sit around, chew the fat, maybe go out to dinner and look over each other's notes, talk about shorthand, talk about the cases we had worked on.

CRAIL: All right. And during that period of time, did you start, at least, to become familiar with his style of writing shorthand?

FRASER: I did.

CRAIL: During that period of time did you ever have occasion to read the notes that Mr. Perry had made, shorthand notes?

FRASER: Yes, I did.

CRAIL: Can you tell us now about how frequently that occurred during your association there at that place?

FRASER: Well, it was quite a few years ago. It would be very difficult to say how frequently, but in the natural course of association, it would be quite frequently.

CRAIL: All right. Could I say this, that you were in daily association with him and in contact with him in connection with your official duties as a court reporter?

FRASER: I was.

CRAIL: And that continued at that place for what period of time?

FRASER: Until the fall of 1919.[3]

CRAIL: What system of shorthand did Mr. Perry write?

FRASER: Mr. Perry wrote a system that was called the Success System. It was promulgated by two men, one named William James, and the other Frederick Rose—I think it was Frederick Rose. Anyway, his last name was Rose. . . . That system was an adaptation of the Graham Pitmanic System. Isaac Pitman was the first Pitman writer, and he used the same alphabet that his brother, who made an adaptation of shorthand from Isaac's system. His name was Ben. There was Isaac Pitman and the Ben Pitman system. They were based upon exactly the same alphabet, and Andrew J. Graham, who was sort of a genius, came along and he made an adaptation from both of those systems, which we call the Graham Pitmanic adaptation of shorthand.

CRAIL: That was the system that Mr. Perry used?

FRASER: Mr. Perry used the Graham Pitmanic as adapted by this Success System, which was promulgated, as I said, by Mr. James and Mr. Rose, in Chicago, where they had a school.

CRAIL: What system have you used, Mr. Fraser?

FRASER: Well, I used the Graham Pitmanic System, G-r-a-h-a-m.

CRAIL: The stenotype reporters[4] don't know those names?

FRASER: Well, it was a little before her time.

CRAIL: All right. And how does your system compare to the system employed by Mr. Perry?

FRASER: They were very close, with the exception—I used some of the Success adaptations of Success outlines; myself, or contractions or expedients that were set forth in the Success System, for I, myself, at one time, having been lured by some publication or some advertisement in regard to the claims made by the—the extraordinary claims made for the Success System—but I wrote Chicago and I got their correspondence lessons and I studied it, myself.

CRAIL: Do you know whether Mr. Perry did or not?

FRASER: Mr. Perry did the same thing.

CHESSMAN:[5] Do you recall what Mr. Leavy said to you at that time?

FRASER: It's quite a long time ago. I couldn't give you the words that he said. As near as I remember, he told me that, he asked me if I knew that Mr. Perry was dead. Well, I told him that I did because I had attended his funeral. Then, he told me that Mr. Perry died before he had completed transcribing his shorthand notes in the trial, *People* against *Chessman*, and that he was trying to find a reporter who was willing and able to make a transcript of Mr. Perry's notes. He told me that he had contacted a number of other official court reporters. I forget how many, and that one of them had told him—I think her name was Mrs. Gurney—that she believed she could make an accurate transcript of those notes, but for one reason or another, she was busy with other matters and she did not wish to undertake it. He said that either he or she had contacted another reporter, I forget his name.

CHESSMAN: Could that have been Mr. Willis N. Tiffany?

FRASER: Yes, it could have been.

CHESSMAN: You're not certain, though?

FRASER: I believe it was now that you refresh my memory. He said he didn't—he said that Mr. Tiffany didn't wish to undertake it. I don't remember that he stated any reason why Mr. Tiffany did not wish to undertake it. He then said that, as I remember it, that he remembered that Mr. Perry had transcribed some of my notes in another criminal case at a time when I was not available to do the work. I forget how many pages there were. There were a couple of hundred pages, maybe more, and I told him that that was true, that Mr. Perry had transcribed several hundred pages, more or less, of my shorthand notes and that I had checked them over and found them to be accurate. He said with that background he thought that—or he wanted to find out whether I would be willing to look at these shorthand notes and determine in my own mind whether I would be able to make a good transcript, an accurate transcript of those notes. Well, I told him that—He also, I think he further said that another reporter or two who had made statements to the effect that Mr. Perry's notes were undecipherable and that they couldn't make head nor tail of them, to use a homely expression. I told him then that I have known Mr. Perry for a great many years and I told him about our association over the years and I said that I didn't believe that his notes were undecipherable. Because I was able to read portions of them without very much study at all at various times through our association together and that I would be willing to look at the notes and I would—he would present them to me and I would let him know in a couple of weeks what my conclusion was as to whether I could make a good transcript of it.

CONCLUDING OBSERVATIONS

It is clear that the account of the friendship between Perry and Fraser had been well rehearsed, including its touching details. Nevertheless, what is important is the fact that Fraser was thoroughly acquainted with the writing style of Perry. This fundamental truth allowed the government to handle many later difficulties.

The Drinking of Stanley Fraser

POSNER:[6] As I started to say previously. Mr. Fraser[7] is a male of approximately 63 years of age. For the major portion of his life he has been a shorthand court reporter. Fraser started drinking in 1927 and along about 1932 or 1935, there were occasions when Fraser would be drunk for two or three days at a time. Between the years of 1940 and 1957, Fraser has been arrested on at least twelve occasions for being drunk or for offenses involving drunkenness. The first arrest occurred in Glendale on January 14, 1940, when Fraser was arrested for driving while intoxicated. The police report for that arrest states as follows:

He was weaving all over the street in a very drunken condition.

The court records show that Fraser pleaded guilty to this-re, rather, strike that. The records will show that the drunk driving was changed to a charge of being plain drunk and Fraser pleaded guilty to that charge and a sentence was imposed. Fraser was given a $150 fine or thirty days and the record shows that the fine was paid.

The second arrest occurred in Glendale on March 5, 1940. This was for being drunk in an auto where the driver, not Fraser, was also drunk. The arrest report states:

> At Glendale and Colorado, where we had been called in to Carpenter's Cafe and told that the above auto just leaving had left without paying for their food and without leaving the food trays . . .

And then I am breaking the quote and the quote will continue:

> . . . found them to be in a drunken condition.

The report further states that the food trays were also found in the car. Fraser pleaded guilty to being drunk and a sentence was imposed. He was given thirty days suspended and placed on a one year probation.

On April 6, 1941, again in Glendale, Fraser was arrested for a third time, this time for drunk driving, and this was approximately one month after his year of probation had ended from his previous arrest. There was an accident and the police report shows that Fraser was arrested at the scene of the accident. He was found intoxicated by the examining physician. Fraser pleaded guilty to this charge and received a sentence. He was fined $150 or given thirty days and the record shows that the fine was paid.

On February 29, 1944, Fraser was arrested for the fourth time, this time for being drunk in Gardena. The arrest report states:

> Observed defendant [Fraser] in the company of blank and blank [two other men] . . . walking north on the sidewalk on the east side of Western Avenue between the Monterey Club and the Gardena Club in an intoxicated condition. Defendant's breath alcoholic, eyes dilated, gait and balance unsteady. Defendant's attitude was stuporous. Brought defendant to station along with above mentioned men and booked as drunk.

Police report further states that:

Found a four-fifths bottle of Three Rivers approximately one-half full.

The disposition of this case has not been found so we don't know whether Fraser was convicted in this charge or not.

For the fifth time Fraser was arrested on April 24, 1945, this time in Los Angeles. He was arrested for being drunk, a misdemeanor. The police report states:

Wandering on street, staggering, unable to take care of himself. Defendant too drunk to care for self.

The disposition of this case also has not been found so we are not able to tell whether Fraser was convicted of this charge or not.

Fraser's sixth arrest occurred in Los Angeles on October 19, 1945. He was arrested for being drunk, a misdemeanor. The police report states:

Defendant down on sidewalk, too drunk to care for self.

The report also states that the defendant admits drinking beer. The disposition of this case has not been found so we are not able to tell whether Fraser was convicted or not.

In 1947 in the month of April, Fraser has a skin rash. He is referred to Dr. Wilhelm, who is a dermatologist. Dr. Wilhelm makes a diagnosis of toxic dermatitis and he states that this toxic dermatitis was due to the chronic drinking of alcoholic beverages, and he has put down on his chart that this was due to the drinking of wine. He classifies Fraser as a wino, and from April 8, 1947 to June 11, 1949, he states that the drinking continued throughout this period.

Between April 8, 1947, to May 23—strike the last statement—Between April 8, 1947, to January 30, 1948, Dr. Wilhelm treated Fraser for this rash and states that although there was some improvement, the rash continued to the last date he treated him.

In 1947, Fraser saw another physician by the name of Dr. James Cryst, who was a general practitioner. Fraser saw this doctor for the first time in December of 1947 and made a statement that he had quit drinking and quit smoking. At this time Fraser complained of dizziness and loss of memory. Between 1947 and 1953, Dr. Cryst treated Fraser for many complaints but never treated him for alcoholism. The doctor stated that he refused to treat Fraser for alcoholism because this was not his type of business. Between 1947 and 1953, it was this doctor's opinion that Fraser was a chronic alcoholic. Fraser was never drunk in his office, but many times would call up and talk to the doctor in an alcoholic state. Fraser's wife complained to the same doctor of Fraser's drinking and the use of physical violence upon her.

For the seventh time Fraser was arrested in Los Angeles on October 21, 1950, this time for being drunk, which is a misdemeanor. The police report states:

> Upon arrival found defendant in living room in a drunken condition. He stated that during a drinking party co-defendant, Helen Arthur, who was very drunk, attempted to sing so he hit her on the head with a telephone. Defendant in a very drunken condition in public view and unable to care for self.

The police report has a statement made by defendant to the police officer which is as follows:

> After we had done quite a bit of drinking she tried to sing and she stinks so I hit her over the head with the phone to quiet her down.

Both Fraser and Helen Arthur were subsequently taken to the Georgia Receiving Hospital where she received treatment for the wound she had suffered on her head. To this charge Fraser pleaded guilty and was given a fine of $25 or five days and the court records show that the fine was paid.

Fraser was arrested for the eighth time in San Diego on March 17, 1951. He was arrested for being drunk. The police report states:

> We were called to the desk of the Grant Hotel regarding drunks. The defendant was on the ramp of the garage where a bottle of

whiskey had been broken on the floor. The defendant was drunk, very loud and making a disturbance.

The police report further shows that his gait was staggering, his speech thick, his breath alcoholic and his eyes bloodshot. Fraser pleaded guilty to this charge and forfeited his bail in the sum of $10.

For the ninth time Fraser was arrested in Whittier on March 25, 1951. He was arrested for drunk driving. The police report states that Fraser was the driver of the car traveling in an erratic manner. It further states:

Found driver, Stanley Fraser, to be intoxicated. Passenger, Mary Helen Arthur, was also intoxicated. Sobriety test given as follows: Balance poor, walk unsteady, speech incoherent, breath had an alcoholic-like odor.

At the time of the trial of this charge, this matter was dismissed in the interests of justice, but we have no records to show why it was so dismissed.

Nine months later on December 21, 1951, Fraser was arrested for drunk driving and being drunk in public. The police report states:

Observed defendant drunk in public view, unable to care for self.

Fraser was found in automobile after an accident. The drunk driving charge was dismissed and Fraser pleaded guilty to being drunk and was fined $50.

On August 13, 1953, Fraser was taken to Los Angeles County General Hospital in a coma after he had taken thirty Iperol tablets and suffered a severe attack of barbiturate intoxication. Fraser was in a coma for twenty-four hours and Fraser was released from the hospital on August 17, 1953. The attending physician, Dr. Lester, noticed:

Marked paranoid delusions. . . . That Mafia is after him, people are plotting against him.

His diagnosis was:

1. Chronic alcoholism
2. Barbiturate overdose
3. Acute brain syndrome secondary to above

The psychiatric consultant at the County Hospital, Dr. Stoller, was told by Fraser that he "has been a heavy drinker, taking one half to one pint of whiskey daily." "Says that just before coming to hospital some men who may be members of Mafia came to his home, wired the room, taped up wife and self, and placed iron bars between them. They did this three times. Patient isn't sure how he got loose. Story that of toxic psychosis, D.T.'s."

Impressions:
1. Acute brain syndrome, D.T.'s cleared.
2. Barbiturate intoxication clearing.

Fraser was arrested for the eleventh time on August 9th—

CRAIL: Pardon me, Mr. Posner, before you pass that. Do you want to include in your question the testimony of Dr. Lester that this brain condition had cleared up before the patient left the hospital and that there was no brain damage found at that time? . . .

POSNER: Fraser was arrested for the eleventh time on August 9, 1954, in Los Angeles, for being drunk in public. He pleaded guilty and was fined $5 or given one day. The records show that he was committed for the one day.

On August 1, 1957, Fraser was arrested in Los Angeles for the twelfth time for being drunk in public. The police report shows:

Drunk in public view, unable to care for self. Breath alcoholic, coordination poor, eyes bloodshot, face flushed, gait staggering, speech incoherent, attitude stuporous.

Fraser pleaded guilty and was sentenced to one day.[8] During the course of this trial eye-witnesses have testified that during the years 1947, 1948, 1949, 1950, 1956, and 1957, they have seen Fraser drunk almost every day. Two persons who sold Fraser liquor between 1947 and 1950 have seen Fraser so drunk that he would at times fall out of his car upon alighting from it and would require assistance in being taken to his room. He was described on occasions as being very drunk. At times he was so intoxicated that the proprietors of a liquor store would refuse to sell him any more liquor. However, he would purchase a pint of whiskey nearly every day. During these three years he lived with a Helen Arthur,[9] a woman not his wife for part of the time, and they were both seen drunk almost every day. They were described on occasions as being so drunk that at times they would make a lavatory out of their car.

Another witness, the manager of an apartment where Fraser lived with the same woman mentioned above, who he had, by this time, married, described Fraser as being drunk almost every day during the years of 1956 and 1957. Before marrying the woman I have previously referred to, Fraser was married before. He had married and remarried his first wife three times, which reasonably implies prior divorces from her. From 1950 on, Fraser was known to inflict bodily harm on his second wife, during occasions when he or both of them were drunk. One such occasion I have previously referred to as taking place on October 21, 1950, when both were arrested and both taken to the County Hospital. His second wife complained of other such occasions to her doctor and other witnesses who have testified. Are there any facts you would like to add, Mr. Crail?

CRAIL: Yes, I think we should let the doctor know that during this entire period of time, Mr. Fraser as you call him, was making his living as a shorthand court reporter in the Superior Court of this county, and that when he was not working as a shorthand reporter in the Superior Court, he was engaged in reading the notes of a deceased reporter that eventually covered some 1800 pages of transcript, and that in the Federal Court in San Francisco, in the years of—in the month January of 1956, he appeared as a witness in this case as he does now.

CHESSMAN: During this period from August of 1948 until the end of the year 1948, will you please describe to me Fraser's actions as you recall them or any incidents that you recall when you observed Mr. Fraser in an intoxicated condition?

SHURE:[10] Well, there would be times when Mr. Fraser would apparently be coming from downtown, park his car in front of the Camp Apartments or in front of our store, open up the door closest to the curb, fall out, his briefcase would be behind him, papers would be strewn all over, and he couldn't get up, so I would either help him get up or if my husband was there, I would ask him to come and help me pick him up, and I would take his papers, put them in his briefcase just helter-skelter, and help him to the door of his apartment so he could walk up the stairs.

There are other times, several occasions, when Mr. Fraser would come in very disheveled and dirty in old clothes and had obviously urinated in his clothing, and there were times when I saw him urinating in the parking lot and then stagger back home.

There are times when he wasn't quite so intoxicated, when he would come in very gay and happily and take off his hat—he wore a hat most often—and bend down and recite poems in Spanish and be very gay.

CHESSMAN: Have you also during this period, or I should say did you also during this period observe the woman you knew as Helen Arthur or Mrs. Helen Fraser in an intoxicated condition?

SHURE: Yes, I have.

CHESSMAN: And during this period from August of 1948 until the end of 1948, were you seeing Mr. Fraser and Helen Arthur Fraser regularly?

SHURE: Yes. As I said, almost every day.

CHESSMAN: I realize that it may be difficult to fix this with certainly after all these years, but are you able to say in any way or fix in any way approximately how often you saw them intoxicated?

SHURE: I would say at least 97 percent of the time.

CHESSMAN: But there were also occasions when you would see them sober?

SHURE: Oh, for a day or two, yes.

CHESSMAN: And what was the manner in which you determined in your opinion that they were intoxicated, Mrs. Shure?

SHURE: Well, by the look of their eyes; they had practically no coordination, they staggered, and they smelled heavily of liquor.

CHESSMAN: And was their speech thick or different?

SHURE: Oh, yes, by all means.

CHESSMAN: Did you ever have any personal knowledge of the police coming to investigate any disturbances during the years 1948, 1949, and 1950?

SHURE: Yes, on several occasions I saw police cars arrive and go upstairs to the apartment and bring down Mr. Fraser and sometimes Mrs. Fraser, take them to the police car. Sometimes they would ask Mr. Fraser to cool off. He would walk over to his—it was in the parking lot—and stay there for several hours, and then come back, take a drink, and go back upstairs.

THE DEFENDANT: I believe I have no further questions.

THE COURT: Cross examine.

CRAIL: You are the daughter of Mrs. Hoffman, who testified here?

SHURE: Yes, I am.

CRAIL: Now, during the period of time that you knew Mr. and Mrs. Fraser, how frequently did you sell liquor to them?

SHURE: Almost every day that they weren't extremely intoxicated.

CRAIL: And that would include the entire period through 1948, 1949, and 1950?

SHURE: That's correct.

CRAIL: Ordinarily, when did they make their purchases; that is, what time of day? Do you remember?

SHURE: Well, if Mr. Fraser wasn't going to the office, as he termed it, it would be as early as 10 o'clock in the morning. On those occasions when Mr. Fraser said he was coming to the office or going to the office, on the time when he would return, and he would usually have had two or three drinks on the way, so he would say, And Mrs. Arthur, those days that she didn't—that she was home, why, it wouldn't be as early as 10 o'clock in the morning.

CRAIL: How many times during the week would you see Mr. Fraser leave, apparently going to work?

SHURE: Well, I wouldn't see him going to work with the exception maybe once or twice during the week.

CRAIL: You wouldn't see him then until—

SHURE: I wouldn't see him that early.

CRAIL: You wouldn't see him then until sometime in the late afternoon: is that correct?

SHURE: Yeah, around 4:30.

CRAIL: Did you notice any difference in the amount of liquor that he was buying during that period of time? In other words, was he buying more during one year than he was the next year?

SHURE: No. It was sort of a constant amount.

CRAIL: And you, of course, never sold liquor to him when he was intoxicated?[11]

SHURE: That is correct.

CHESSMAN: Now, at the time that you were settling this transcript, or any time prior to the time you were settling the transcript, did you know that Mr. Fraser had a record of arrests for being drunk or for being drunk in an automobile or for drunken driving?

FRICKE: Assuming that he had such a record, I didn't know of it.

CHESSMAN: Specifically, it was never called to your attention, Judge Fricke, that Mr. Stanley Fraser was arrested on January 14, 1940, in Glendale, for violation of Section 502 of the Vehicle Code; that he was arrested on March 5, 1940, for being drunk in an automobile—and that also was in Glendale; that he was arrested on April 6, 1941, for a violation of Section 501 of the Vehicle Code—that also was in Glendale. . .

FRICKE: I can save you some time, Mr. Chessman, by saying that I had no information which would indicate that Mr. Fraser had ever been arrested for anything, until after the transcript was settled and certified. In other words, I didn't know it until after the appeal had been perfected, and then my only knowledge came by way of hearsay.

CHESSMAN: Well, the records in evidence before this court, Judge Fricke, show that Mr. Fraser was arrested, on several occasions, in Gardena, in Glendale, and in Los Angeles County, as well as other places, for drunkenness, for being drunk in an automobile, or for drunken driving. And if that information had come to your attention at the time of the settlement of the transcript, do you feel that it would have had any influence whatever upon your ultimately approving this transcript?

FRICKE: There is a mere possibility. However, I will say the test that I would apply would be not whether he had been arrested for taking too much liquor on some occasion or occasions, but whether he could properly translate the notes.

CHESSMAN: And you wouldn't feel that even though he might have been intoxicated during the time that he was actually preparing this record, that that, in itself, would be a bar to him accepting. . .

FRICKE: I had no information, and I have never heard any insinuation that he was intoxicated at the time he prepared the record. The fact that the man has been intoxicated or even arrested for being intoxicated doesn't necessarily mean that he is incapable, on other occasions—I think we have some very prominent characters in history who were noted for their overindulgence in liquor, and still they were among our great men of great ability.

CHESSMAN: The records here, Judge Fricke, show that the reporter's transcript in augmentation of the record on appeal, which contained the *voi dire* examination of jurors and the prosecutor's opening address, was prepared from August 7, 1950, until January 11, 1951, which is while Mr. Fraser was actually engaged in preparing this reporter's transcript in augmentation of the record, he was arrested and jailed for being drunk.

FRICKE: If that is—was all, no, because the mere fact that a person is arrested doesn't show that he is guilty of anything.

CHESSMAN: If it was shown that the police officers were, or if, I say, if the police officers' testimony or statements, I should say, at the time that the arrest was made, and if this statement was verified by the police officers, or stipulated to by prosecution to be correct, do you believe that you would have conducted an investigation? And I will read you the statement:

Approximately 2:52 P.M. this date received call, "cutting." Upon arrival found defendant in kitchen bleeding freely from an open wound on top rear portion of head. Defendant stated that during an argument, she was struck on the head by co-defendant, Stanley Fraser, booking number 50934, with the telephone receiver.

Defendant was treated at the scene by unit C-7 and transported to Georgia Receiving Hospital with co-defendant for further treatment.

Received treatment for deep laceration rear top portion of head; dressed; stitched and cleansed by Dr. Miller. Advised own doctor.

Defendant was in an intoxicated condition and was using loud profanity in presence of other women and small children. Defendant was unable to care for herself after being in view of public. Booked as above.

Defendant was arrested in front of 3515 West Pico in view of crowd that had assembled.

And then it says that, just above, she made this statement at the time of arrest, attributed to Mrs. Helen Fraser or Helen Arthur, as she is also known:

We were sitting around drinking, so I started to sing Irish songs and he didn't like it and hit me on the head with the telephone.

Now, if that information had been brought to you, do you believe that you would have conducted an investigation?

FRICKE: If that was the only information, no. I think before I would conduct an investigation, or before I'd be inclined to conduct an investigation, I'd want to have something to show a relationship between an incident of that sort and the preparation of the transcript, which might be affected by it.

CHESSMAN: Well, that is the point I am trying to determine is, if you wouldn't have investigated to find out if there were a relationship, or do you feel that the burden would be on someone else and that if this, even though the matter might have been called to your attention, that you wouldn't investigate until someone else was in a position to prove conclusively. . .

FRICKE: No, I—the mere fact that someone was acting as transcriber transcribing a reporter's notes at some time had gotten into a situation where she got hit over the head with a telephone and was intoxicated. . .

CHESSMAN: By the person doing the transcribing.

FRICKE: No, I think it was the reverse, wasn't it?[12]

CHESSMAN: By the person doing the dictating?

FRICKE: Yes. I think I'd want some information to indicate that it had some relationship or bearing upon the transcription.

CHESSMAN: And you would feel that that type of person who drank and quarreled with the person doing the deciphering and who was living with the person doing the deciphering and who was profane in the presence of women and children and who was using alcohol to excess during this period, would not in itself throw any question in your mind, or any doubt in your mind upon the competency of both the transcriber and the person doing the deciphering?

FRICKE: Not by itself. I'd want to have some information that it had a relationship to the preparation of the transcript.

CRAIL:[13] I am not going to attempt to tell Your Honor that Mr. Fraser didn't have a drinking problem. I have endeavored throughout this hearing to be as fair as I could with Your Honor and with the defendant, and I certainly recognize the fact that he did have a drinking problem. I suppose we could say the same thing about General Grant. If my memory serves me correctly, I think he was dismissed from the Army while he was stationed here in California because he was driving a team of horses in one of our small cities while intoxicated. And yet we know that he was a brilliant individual.

Bringing it closer to home, let me cite the case of Earl Rodgers, probably the greatest criminal lawyer we have ever had west of the Mississippi. I don't know what his count is but I think he defended some forty individuals accused of murder and never had one of them suffer the death penalty. Yet I am not speaking of him disrespectfully when I say that throughout that period of time, time and again his cases were postponed because he was in no condition to try them.

I might also refer to Stephen M. White, whose statue stands down there on Broadway with his arms raised in a speaking gesture. I remember a bailiff here some years ago who worked in a livery stable that was down on First and Broadway, known as the Tally-ho. He has told me of instances when he would go to a saloon on Main Street and pick up Mr. White in a helpless condition and take him home because he was intoxicated, and that that same Mr. White would be in court the following day trying a lawsuit.

These or others are evidently the individuals that Judge Fricke had in mind when he was testifying here on this witness stand.

The work that Mr. Fraser has done speaks louder than any number of witnesses they might bring in here. Imagine an individual sitting down and trying to transcribe those notes while he was intoxicated! Imagine an individual being able to write that fine copybook shorthand that appears throughout the notes in Mr. Fraser's penciled writing!

CONCLUDING OBSERVATIONS

It seems impossible that as heavy a drinker as Fraser could perform the delicate transcription necessary. Expert testimony asserts that he did, so does his coherence at the 1957 hearing. Thus he either was telling the truth when he claimed the transcription was done during a dry spell, or he is one of the rare few stimulated rather than hindered by alcoholic consumption. In either case his drinking appears to be irrelevant. The flamboyant testimony of Mrs. Shure must be regarded as exaggerated.

15

The Family Relationship between Leavy and Fraser

CHESSMAN: You are related to Mr. Leavy, are you, Mr. Fraser?

FRASER: Yes.

CHESSMAN: By marriage?

FRASER: Yes.

CHESSMAN: You're the uncle-in-law by marriage or the uncle-in-law, I'll say, of Mr. Leavy; is that correct?

FRASER: Yes. They had been married eighteen years when this hearing was held up in San Francisco.[14]

CHESSMAN: So that they had been . . .

FRASER: That was 1956, so obviously they were.

CHESSMAN: They had been married for several years, then?

FRASER: Yes.

CHESSMAN: When you undertook this work and when Mr. Leavy first contacted you in July of 1948 at Long Beach: is that correct?

FRASER: Oh, yes.

CHESSMAN: Now, during the time that the negotiations were being had for this contract, did you ever tell Judge Fricke or the Board of Supervisors of County Counsel that you were related by marriage to Mr. Leavy?

FRASER: It didn't occur to me that it was necessary. I thought everybody in the Hall of Justice knew about it because my niece had been secretary to the chief of the Bureau of Investigation in the District Attorney's office down there for a number of years.

CRAIL: Well, I take it from the answer that he didn't tell anyone.

FRASER: I don't remember whether I told anyone or not. I don't think I did. It didn't occur to me.

CHESSMAN: And, up until the time that this transcript—these first five volumes[15] I am referring to now—had been prepared by yourself and settled and approved by Judge Fricke, on June 1, 2, 3, 1949, did you ever during that intervening period, tell the parties mentioned in the last question that you were related by marriage to Mr. Leavy?

FRASER: I don't believe I did. I don't recall it.

CHESSMAN: At the time that this transcript was actually settled on June 1, 2, and 3, 1949, and more specifically, at the time that you testified, on June 1, 1949, did you tell Judge Fricke that you were related, by marriage, to Mr. Leavy?

CRAIL: I will stipulate he never told anyone, at any time, if that will get us along over this . . . with the possible exception of Judge Goodman, I think, in San Francisco, when the question was asked of him.

CONCLUDING OBSERVATIONS

Nepotism is always a sticky issue. We know that a lot of politicians hire members of their families, or see that they are taken care of. And often that's legitimate. In this case, Fraser was uncle by marriage to Leavy, the thinnest of connections. Leavy and Fraser had both worked in the same courtroom many times before. No one else ever challenged it and in any other case it would have been laughed off. There are indications that Chessman was informed in 1948 about the Fraser-Leavy relationship, not by Leavy as perhaps should have been the case, but by the wife of his legal advisor, Al Matthews. If the relationship bothered Chessman, he could have complained immediately in one of his endless number of petitions. He waited half a dozen years to do so. Courts would be most understandably less receptive to his claims when he was so slow in making it. The final telling point that favors the prosecution on this point is that if the notes of Perry were always available to read by any other expert who could do so, any attempt at fraud stood a chance of being detected.

16

Possible Collusion between Prosecution and Police

CHESSMAN: Now, in addition to using the first three volumes of the record which Mr. Fraser—I mean Mr. Perry had dictated, and which was transcribed by Miss Grace Petermichael, did you use any other aids in preparing your transcript of volumes 4 to 8 inclusive, of this reporter's transcript, as well as the one volume in augmentation of the record?

FRASER: Oh, yes.

CHESSMAN: Will you please tell the Court what they are and were?

FRASER: Well, I had a photostatic copy of Judge Fricke's rather voluminous note; longhand notes, and I also had the Clerk's roster of witnesses and exhibits, and I also got whatever light I could on places where I had difficulty in making a transcription, from whatever sources were available to me.

CHESSMAN: And what were those sources you found available to you?

FRASER: Well, I went down to the Criminal Laboratory, which was down on First and Hill, in the old Police Building, to talk to Lieutenant Leland Jones, who was the head of the laboratory at that time.

CHESSMAN: Did you do so at anyone's suggestion, Mr. Fraser?

FRASER: No, I went on my own hook.

CHESSMAN: You went down there strictly on your own, and specifically, Mr. Leavy didn't suggest to you to go down there?

LEAVY:[16] One reason, so far as Leland Jones was concerned, he testified concerning the identity of hair of Mary Alice Meza, from her head, and some hair that was found in the car in which you were arrested, and knowing that that type of testimony is a certin type of testimony Mr. Lee Jones, if he testified, would remember the vernacular which he used, in that way, he would know whether Mr. Perry properly reported it and whether Fraser had properly read it. As to Mr. Colin Forbes, I knew that Mr. Colin Forbes had, when testifying, used his police reports and notes concerning his conversations on other matters about which he testified, and Mr. Colin Forbes could tell, from what Perry had, from Perry's notes, whether Perry had properly reported him, as well as whether Fraser had properly read Perry's notes. Those are the circumstances.

CHESSMAN: Did you tell Judge Fricke about these two talks?

LEAVY: I am not certain. I could have.

CHESSMAN: In any other case or any other criminal case, I should say, in which you have been the prosecutor, have you ever had a court reporter bring rough drafts of the transcription of what he was doing to you to be checked?

LEAVY: I have, many times, had court reporters come to me, before they completed their transcripts, both daily and on appeal, and check with me concerning something that I may have said, before they, in the final analysis, prepare their transcript and certify to it.

CHESSMAN: Have you ever had them bring rough drafts to you?

LEAVY: They may have brought the transcript, at that place when it wasn't completed. If you want to call that a rough draft, it is a rough draft.

CHESSMAN: Well, I can assure you I don't want to call it anything, Mr. Leavy. I am merely trying to get at the facts here.

CHESSMAN: Well, I think that the circumstances in this case, as you no doubt will recall, are that there is—there is—Mr. Forbes gave testimony of what was characterized as an oral confession, as well as some admissions against interest. And, if you, taking that into account—if you had known that Mr. Fraser, in attempting to prepare a transcript from a dead reporter's notes had gone to see a man or prosecution witness with regard to such testimony, do you feel that would have merited an investigation?

FRICKE: I don't think you got the effect of my last answer. It would depend upon what he went to see him for. For example, I recall one peculiar circumstance that someone, during the trial, referred to a gun as being a .46 caliber. I can see, if I were a reporter and were going over notes and saw "forty-six caliber" in the notes, I would say, "Well, there is something wrong here,"—if that reporter then went to the witness and asked him about it and the witness said, "Yes, that is what I said," I wouldn't see anything particular present in that situation to cause any comment or question.

CONCLUDING OBSERVATIONS

This is another smoke screen. It sounds bad, but in reality it appears to be quite innocent and praiseworthy. Clearly the notes of Perry were difficult to read. Consultation with certain principals as to their recollection is not out of place, but shows, on the contrary devotion to duty. As always, the Perry notes were there as a backstop. Fraser, Leavy and the policemen didn't get together, open a bottle of beer and make up their own trial transcript.

In early 1949, Chessman was given the opportunity to read the Fraser transcription before Judge Fricke certified it as being accurate. This was the time for him to point out major errors. All his suggested corrections were small and did not change the substance of the transcript. The procedure did not run afoul of the United States Supreme Court because of any failure to give

Chessman timely opportunity to object to errors in the Fraser transcription. The Supreme Court objected to the fact he was required to do so in writing and was not allowed to appear before Fricke, either personally or with counsel, to contest in person the adequacy of the Fraser transcription.

17

The Quality of the Perry Notes

FRASER: From my comparison of Mr. Perry's transcript with Mr. Perry's notes—I mean the portion of Mr. Perry's notes that Mr. Perry transcribed before he died, I would say that Mr. Perry's transcript, as filed in this case, is a true and accurate transcript of his notes.

CHESSMAN: If all the changes and corrections which you have felt should be made were to appear in the transcript, do you believe that you could certify it as a true and accurate transcript of the proceedings of the Chessman trial?

LILL:[17] I believe that I could certify it as a transcript between 98 and 99 percent accurate.

CHESSMAN: And you, of course, have no way of knowing, when you say that, if Mr. Perry actually recorded all of the proceedings?

LILL: I have no way of knowing, but I have a very good way of inferring.

CHESSMAN: Would you please explain?

LILL: If a reporter misses things, it is evident in his notes, to me. You can't leave out proceedings without breaking continuity, to any extent.

CHESSMAN: Do you have any recollection of reading about the case from time to time or discussing it with anyone?

LILL: I am sure that I read about it from time to time casually.

CHESSMAN: And do you recall discussing it with anyone?

LILL: No, I do not.

CHESSMAN: You have stated, I believe, that with the corrections you would make or that you suggest in your findings, that this transcript would be among the top 97 to 98 percent; is that correct, in terms of accuracy, in completeness?

LILL: Well, I didn't say it would be among the top. I said that I believe it would be within about that percent of an accurate transcript.

CHESSMAN: Basing your answer exclusively on what you find in Mr. Perry's notes?

LILL: Yes.

CHESSMAN: Would you call the first three volumes of the reporter's transcript, as prepared by Mr. Perry, from his own notes, and dictated by him before his death, true and accurate transcription?

LILL: There, again, I would say that if I had considered it absolutely accurate, I would not have made any changes in it. I don't remember the number that I did suggest in there, but it impressed me as a reasonably good transcript and a fair transcript. I found nothing in any portion of it which seemed to be unfair or changing meanings.

FRICKE: I understand that, subsequent to the settlement of the transcript, certain reporters came out and said that they couldn't interpret the notes which had no effect upon me at all, because I couldn't have interpreted them, myself. It would require somebody familiar with the science to be able to do it.

CHESSMAN: But, prior to the settlement of the transcript, were you ever informed that reporters were not capable of reading Mr. Perry's notes with sufficient accuracy to prepare a transcription?

FRICKE: I don't recall that, Mr. Chessman, but if some reporter had told me that he could not interpret Mr. Perry's notes, either with or without accuracy, I wouldn't have paid any attention to it, because the fact that he was unable to do so wouldn't show that somebody else was not able to do so.

SMITH:[18] How would you describe the transcript in terms of accuracy?

BURDICK:[19] It was a very accurate transcript, as transcripts are judged and filed day after day.

SMITH: Now, Mr. Burdick, how would you compare this transcript with other transcripts filed in cases in Los Angeles County?

BURDICK: At least the top three percent in accuracy and care of—putting it together.

SMITH: Did you find that this transcript was substantially true and correct as a reflection of Mr. Perry's notes?

BURDICK: Permit me just a second. Yes, substantially. There was one place in there where I think Mr. Perry must have, when putting in one of the volumes, where Judge Fricke was explaining to the jury what their duties were before they started the selection, you see, and the notes that we had there, oh, they were substantially the same but there were little differences and I think he put, he accidentally perhaps picked up a copy that had been used many times. But it contained substantially the same matter. Outside of that, I think it was almost word for word.

SMITH: Now, Mr. Burdick, after examining Mr. Perry's notes, what did you conclude in regard to their readability. Did you decide, determine that they were readable?

BURDICK: They are readable, and very readable to a person who writes the style that he does.

SMITH: Now, Mr. Burdick, do you feel that if you were given the first 650 pages which were transcribed by Mr. Perry and adequate time to study that part of the transcription, that you would be able to prepare a transcript yourself from these notes?

BURDICK: Oh, yes, I have had jobs that were more difficult than that and almost as big, and with *almost* no error at all.

DAVIS:[20] Mr. Burdick, what did you mean when you said Mr. Perry had a dashing style?

BURDICK: I would say that he took his writing tool, pencil or pen, much after this style (indicating) and rolled his hand kind of across the page. I have been told that that is what he did, though I never was with him but once when he was writing shorthand, and I don't remember. I was in court once taking his place in Judge Fricke's court.

DAVIS: Stanley Fraser told you that he had a dashing style?

BURDICK: Yes, where he kind of rolled his hand like that, you see. There are some writers that do that, and it is a hand motion as contradistinguished from a finger motion. Stanley has just the opposite. He had a fine finger motion where his pen would be almost vertical. He would just roll along, go along smoothly like that. You can hardly see it move.

DAVIS: Would a reporter who used a dashing style be more likely to write notes difficult to read?

BURDICK: Oh, yes.

DAVIS: Than the other kind of reporter?

BURDICK: Oh, yes, yes, because when the speakers, as we say, pour it on and go fast, they have got to readjust their hand as they go along, you see. There will be little starts and stops and there will be some motions—every time that he has had the word "cross examination" he has a huge M stroke. It is much easier to do that, you see.

DAVIS: Yes?

BURDICK: Twice as big as necessary.

DAVIS: Yes. And where this use of the dashing style occurs in the course of fast writing, fast reporting, it would be more difficult for someone trying to read those notes, because the reporter's notes would be less decipherable; is that right?

BURDICK: That's right.

DAVIS: And if the reporter used the dashing style to the extreme, it would result in notes, in part at least, where only he would be able to decipher them, because he would remember what he was doing?

BURDICK: Well, in spots, perhaps, that may be true. Very limited places, though.

CHESSMAN:[21] The letter is dated September 16th, 1948. It is addressed to:

Board of Supervisors of Los Angeles County,
Hall of Records,
Los Angeles 12, California.

ATTENTION: Hon. Raymond V. Darby, Chairman.

Gentlemen:
On motion of our Executive Committee and in accordance with public policy, we are writing this letter to your honorable Board.

It has been brought to our attention through publicity contained in the legal journals that your Board has had under consideration the signing of a contract with a Los Angeles County court reporter covering the transcription of the shorthand notes of one of our deceased members, Ernest R. Perry, taken in the case of People versus Caryl Chessman, No. 117963 and 117964

Inasmuch as the tenor of this publicity is that you are 'reluctantly' obligating the County to pay a minimum fee of $6,000.00 on behalf of the Official Corps of Reporters of the Superior Court, may we respectfully present the following matters:

We believe the purported charge against the County is not only an exorbitant one per se, but will reflect further adverse publicity upon our group, because we have serious doubts that any reporter will be able to furnish a usable transcription of said shorthand notes. Other reporters of our number have examined and studied Mr. Perry's notes and have reached the conclusion that many portions of the same will be found completely indecipherable because toward the latter part of each court session, Mr. Perry's notes show his illness. We feel that this should be brought to your attention.

Sincerely and respectfully,
EXECUTIVE COMMITTEE Of The LOS ANGELES
SUPERIOR COURT REPORTERS' ASSOCIATION.

By: HARRY R. PERSON.

CHESSMAN: And you recognize this letter as having been written by yourself; is that correct, Mr. Person?
PERSON: The letter was not dictated by myself. The committee, consisting of myself and Willis N. Tiffany and Monroe Conlee were the ones that considered the matter. I was of a

different opinion than the other two members of the committee. But, as the chairman of the committee, I had to sign the letter.

HANNA:[22] When I first began to examine the notes I noted that I could readily read many of the outlines just at a glance and the notes seemed to be fairly well written.

CHESSMAN: Now, when you say you began, you are referring to the beginning of the trial proceedings as they were recorded by Mr. Perry?

HANNA: That is right, at the beginning of the first notebook and for some time thereafter. And I at that time did not anticipate that I would have much difficulty in reading the notes, after studying his style for a while.

Later on I found that the notes seemed to progressively deteriorate and become much more less easily read; that a great many of the outlines were so distorted or shattered as to be completely illegible to me, and I found erratic variations from the established rules of writing Pitmanic shorthand, even to the extent of writing strokes in the wrong direction, which would have a different signification; and of writing, for example, half-length strokes as full-length strokes, and very often a stroke which should have been straight was curved or one which should have been curved was straight, altering the meaning of the symbol entirely. And in many places the circles and hooks were imperfectly formed, which made it more difficult to read the notes readily, and in cases impossible for me to decipher the outline at all.

In a few cases he even put circles and hooks on the wrong side of the stroke, a most elementary error, which I am confident Mr. Perry could not have done if he had been in normal possession of his faculties or if something hadn't happened to impair his mental processes and coordination.

CHESSMAN: I see. And you have spelled out in some detail the basis for your findings or your beliefs as they are indicated in Defendant's Y for identification and, based upon your study of the notes themselves, why you believe there was something wrong in the sense of—when I say something wrong, something that was impairing Mr. Perry's ability or efficiency to record these proceedings; is that correct? You have so indicated in your findings?

HANNA: That is correct. I was really perplexed as I went along by the inconsistencies in his writing methods and by the malformation and distortion of the notes; in many instances greater than I have ever noticed before in reporters' notes.

Very frequently it happens in rapidly written shorthand that the notes are not perfectly executed, because different writers have certain idiosyncracies in their writing style. But usually those variations from the perfect outlines follow a certain pattern, so that the notes may be perfectly legible even though they are not executed with perfect accuracy. I found that not to be true with Mr. Perry's notes, because the errors in execution which I found didn't follow any pattern at all. They were just erratic and inexplicable to me and often made the meaning of the notes problematical, and great uncertainty as to what was intended to be written.

CHESSMAN: And I note here from your findings in People's Y for identification that you state that Mr. Perry wrote a simple, rather elementary style of shorthand and failed to avail himself of many of the special word signs and contractions and expedients used normally by skilled reporters.

Would this slow down his top reporting speed? And I mean would it impair his ability to write at greater speeds?

HANNA: It definitely would. He wrote a very simple style, using a few of the contractions and expedients which all reporters use, and especially in criminal cases where the terminology is quite susceptible to that kind of contraction.

CHESSMAN: So that, for example, if you came across a symbol with an "N" stroke and then a loop or a circle, you would be obliged more or less to take your choice and decide from the context again what Mr. Perry intended; that it would be difficult if not impossible to be certain from the symbols themselves; is that correct?

HANNA: That is true. I was mystified as I went along in the case to account for these basic departures from the established methods of writing, knowing Mr. Perry to have been an experienced reporter and believing him to be a capable reporter, as he had a high reputation with his fellow reporters, including myself. I was at a loss to understand how these things could be happening in his shorthand, and some time before I finish my testimony I would like to comment on that a little further.

CHESSMAN: All right.

HANNA: In other words, I might say at this time that it would certainly be very repugnant to me to be placed in the odious position of criticizing a man who is not here to defend himself because I knew him personally and he was a very fine gentleman and of high standing with his fellow reporters, and I am sure that if he had not been a capable reporter, an eminent jurist like Judge Fricke would not have retained him as the Official Reporter of his court for years. So that in any of my criticisms of his shorthand in this case, I would like to have it definitely understood that I am not reflecting upon his ability as a reporter, until I came to examine his notes in this case, when I was at a loss to account for what I found.

CHESSMAN: And you found them written, as you have indicated, with a disregard for the elementary rules and the principles which would make for decipherability; is that correct, in this case?

HANNA: Yes, decidedly so, even to the extent where in a few instances, not in a great many, but in some I found the type of errors you would expect in a student beginning the study of shorthand, where a hook was placed on the wrong side of a stroke, for instance, or a stroke was struck in the reverse of the proper angle, and elementary errors of that sort which I felt confident Mr. Perry could not have been guilty of if he had been in the full normal possession of his faculties. I was at a loss to account for it.

CRAIL: All right. So when you started on Volume 4[23] you had none of the testimony in your mind that had gone before that, when you began your work; is that correct?

HANNA: That is true, except the testimony in the transcript in augmentation.

CRAIL: All right. As a reporter, do you believe that you might have been aided by the context and content of the first three volumes before you tackled Volume 4?

HANNA: Ultimately it might possibly have been of some assistance. Of course, I did later read the preceding three volumes; so that ultimately I have the complete context in my mind.

CRAIL: Well, after having read the first three volumes, did you then go over Volume 4 again?

HANNA: No.

CRAIL: Did you go over Volume 5 again?

HANNA: No.

CRAIL: 6 or 7?

HANNA: I had no occasion. I didn't go over any of the other volumes a second time.

CONCLUDING OBSERVATIONS

This comes down to a fielder's choice. Do you believe Mrs. Lill or Mr. Hanna? Someone is wrong. The reader is handicapped in making a decision. His evaluation of the judgment of the two experts is necessarily limited to the small amount of testimony furnished in this book. Space and relative importance necessitated these condensations. For what it is worth, let me offer my evaluation of the full testimony of Hanna and Lill as contained in the 6,000-page transcript.

To me, Mrs. Lill wins hands down. She had a grasp of courtroom conditions that Mr. Hanna seemed to lack. Her testimony took into account the difficulty of working under pressure. It also considered the fact that Perry wrote these notes for his own eyes only. He naturally used shortcuts that others would find difficult to fathom. Hanna treated the whole thing like a classroom exercise. The vagueness of some of his answers caused his whole testimony to ring false somehow. It does seem his study was not as extensive as the seriousness of the matter warranted.

18

The Quality of the Fraser Transcript

CHESSMAN: And you have indicated that many of these words could stand for several other different words, from the manner in which they are executed?

LEAVY:[24] You mean symbols?

CHESSMAN: Yes, I do. I beg your pardon.

CHESSMAN: That many of these symbols—for example, the word "time" with just an "m," and some of these others, such as the symbol for "that" or "this" or prepositions. Now, Mrs. Kalin, if one word had been misread or mistranscribed, what consequences, in your opinion, might flow in the reading of following words?

KALIN:[25] All the words could be misread.

Just to give you an example, a symbol such as "m," what it could stand for, I can't think of them offhand but here is a book of reporting—they call them logograms, and I will read you some of the words that one symbol could stand for. A symbol such as a little stroke like this, a "p," could stand for "p," "pie," "weep," "pay," "ape," "up," "payee," "hope," "party," "pa," like father, "pew," "happy."

By putting a little "s" on the word something like this (indicating), it would stand for "piece," "poise," "pies," "peace," "paws," "pies," "weeps," "peas," "pace," "pose," "oppose," "pus," "opus," "compass," "compose," "pass," "post," "parties."

Now, by putting a little hook, the word would then stand for "opposition," "apposition," "position," "composition," "possession."

Now, by putting a larger "s" on the word—incidentally, this is not a complete list. This is just what is in the book. There are other words people could think of. By making a larger "s" on the "p" it would stand for "pieces," "pauses," "appeases," It could stand for "appease his," or "appease us," "possess." Of course, the "his" and an "us," it could stand for anything as long as the context makes sense. For instance, besides "appease his" or "appease us," it could stand for "possess his" or "possess us." It could stand for "paces," "poses," "opposes." It could stand for "pace his," "pace us," "oppose his," "oppose us." It could stand for "passes," it could stand for "pass his," "pass us," "hopes his."

Now, by making a little change here (indicating), making it an "s" hook with this type of a shape, it could stand for "pieced," "weepest," "paced," "post," "pest," "compassed," "past," "passed." That's p-a-s-t and p-a-s-s-e-d. "Happiest."

By making a little larger circle it would stand for "poster," "pester," "pastor." It could also stand for "pasture."

By not closing the circle up and just putting a little hook on it, it would stand for "poverty," "pave," "puff." It could stand for "hope to have," the contraction.

By changing the hook and putting it on the other side, which makes it an "n" hook instead of an "f" or "v" hook, it would stand for "pawn," "pin," "pine," " upon," "pain," p-a-i-n, "pane," p-a-n-e, "pen," "pun," "open."

It is a contraction for "punish" or "punishment." It is a contraction for "happen."

By closing this little "n" hook it could stand for "pawns," "pins," "pines," "pin his," "pin us," "pawn his," "pawn us," "peace," "pains," "opens," "pounce," "punishes," "punishments," "punish his," "punish us."

By putting a little hook after the "n-s," which puts a "shun" into it, it would stand for words like "compensation," and what else—

By putting a little hook on the "shun" hook, which would make it look like a small "m-t," it would stand for "appeasement." It could stand for any word with the "m-t" added onto the words I have already given you.

CHESSMAN: And by the addition of these various circles and loops and hooks, Mrs. Kalin, is this true of other consonants, too?

KALIN: It is a principle that is used all through Pitmanic shorthand.

CRAIL: What about the balance of the volumes there you prepared?

FRASER: I would say the same about the balance.

CRAIL: And what do you say?

FRASER: I would say that it is a substantially true and accurate verbatim transcript of Mr. Perry's notes.

FRASER: There are words that I couldn't transcribe at that time, that caused me to condense it, because of—well, that caused me to condense it. But I can read them now.

CHESSMAN: Well, in preparing this transcript, Mr. Fraser, did you feel, or did you believe, that you were free to exercise a discretion in whether or not you should condense questions and answers?

FRASER: Well, Mr. Chessman, I was not employed to furnish an absolute verbatim, word-for-word transcript. I was employed to furnish a transcript that I believed substantially reflected the facts of the proceedings.

CHESSMAN: And so you felt that that left you free to exercise a discretion with respect, for example, to compressing questions and answers?

FRASER: In a very limited way, naturally.

CHESSMAN: And you also felt that where you found that Mr.

Perry had skeletonized his notes that you were free to add in the words that you felt were said at the trial?

FRASER: Well, I did the very best I could, Mr. Chessman, to produce the very best record that I could, and I did not believe that it was up to me to have the last say on whether the transcript was substantially true and accurate.

CHESSMAN: All right. Will you turn, please, to page 124 of the notes?

FRASER: Your Honor, if I might add a word of explanation to that answer, I believe that many shorthand reporters use abbreviated sentences, leaving out connecting words in many instances, which they supply when they make the transcription, because the words are indicated by the context. I have done this in quite a number of instances in order to make the record—I believed that Mr. Perry would have, indicated by what he had dictated previously in this case.

CHESSMAN: Did you also believe that while Mr. Perry may have dictated it that way that those were actually the words that were said at the trial?

FRASER: Yes, I think that's true.

CHESSMAN: What, from the context, led you to believe, for example, that the word, "sufficient," had been said by Mr. Leavy?

FRASER: Mr. Leavy was the Deputy District Attorney in the court, criminal court in which I worked for ten years, oh, for approximately a year, two years maybe; maybe more, maybe less. [26] And I was very familiar with the manner of speaking of Mr. Leavy and I just believed that those words indicated that that was what Mr. Leavy said. And knowing Mr. Leavy's habit of speaking very, very, very rapidly, not drawing a breath or pausing between sentences, paragraphs, or even where he made a start to ask a question or to make a statement, either in argument or in asking a question, without changing pace at all or indicating a pause or stopping for breath, he would start off on an entirely different slant, or entirely new question or new statement, which sometimes would do some violence to the reporter, because he had to write those words down in the sequence in which they were uttered. And Mr. Leavy was very difficult to write for that reason. Being very familiar with Mr. Leavy's manner of delivery and his manner of questions, his manner of argument, I believed that those words were omitted by Mr. Perry from what Mr. Leavy actually did say, in that particular instance.

CHESSMAN: Mr. Leavy never actually told you, though, that those were the words that he had said?

FRASER: No.

CHESSMAN: Did you ever, in the course of preparing this transcript, ever ask Mr. Leavy in any instances where words of Mr. Perry's symbols for words apparently were not complete, and you were required to supply some further words, did you ever ask Mr. Leavy what he had said?

FRASER: I don't remember doing that, but I will say this, I do remember asking Mr. Leavy if he—When I had some difficulty with some outlines that I was unable to transcribe at the moment, I have read to him what I was able to transcribe and ask him if he remembered what he said at that particular point and I will say, further, that very rarely, if ever, do I remember that Mr. Leavy was able to assist me in that respect.[27]

CHESSMAN: And when you had familiarized yourself with Mr. Perry's current shorthand penmanship, did you find that it differed in any way from the penmanship you had examined at any time earlier?

FRASER: Not substantially.

CHESSMAN: He was writing essentially the same system when he reported the proceedings of the Chessman trial in 1948 as he was writing when you examined his notes, say, between these periods of 1914 and 1919, and 1932 and 1938 or 1939; is that correct?

FRASER: I would say his penmanship was substantially the same, or similar.

CHESSMAN: How did you go about making this check of the first three volumes of the transcript?

FRASER: Well, as I told you, my wife would read from the

transcript to me and I would follow Mr. Perry's notes as she read it.

CHESSMAN: Did you find places where Mr. Perry had failed to transcribe any of his own symbols?

FRASER: I don't remember.

CHESSMAN: Did you find places where the notes did not coincide, in your opinion, with the transcript as Mr. Perry had prepared?

FRASER: There may have been a few instances of that kind.

CHESSMAN: When you encountered an instance of these pencilled notations of yours, did you transcribe Mr. Perry's symbol?

FRASER: I transcribed Mr. Perry's symbol at all times.

CHESSMAN: Well, then, how did placing these pencilled symbols of your own in Mr. Perry's notebook for future reference help you in the transcription?

FRASER: Well, it wasn't very often that Mr. Perry's symbols differed from mine. There may have been—there were undoubtedly a number of cases where that occurred, but I soon became familiar through studying Mr. Perry's notes, with the difference between the forms, the symbols that he used and the symbols which I used which meant the same thing, and that's what I mean when I say that I had transcribed Mr. Perry's symbols in each case.

CHESSMAN: When you later actually did the transcribing work and you were dictating or typing or however you were doing it, you always and invariably referred to Mr. Perry's symbols and never to your pencilled additions; is that correct?

FRASER: Well, if I said that, it isn't exactly correct. What I mean is that I could dictate direct from Mr. Perry's notes, long portions of his shorthand, after I became familiar with them, after studying them over times and times, dozens of times in some instances reading them over, and sometimes I would put my own shorthand symbols there so that I wouldn't, in case I should forget the difference in the symbol, so that I wouldn't have to lose any time on figuring it over, until I became more familiar with his shorthand symbols.

CHESSMAN: And until you became more familiar, you were adding pencilled additions; is that correct?

FRASER: Yes, and even after that, I think, in some instances.

CHESSMAN: And did you find Mr. Fraser's transcription of Volume 4 to 8 inclusive, and the reporter's transcript in augmentation of the record on appeal, a true and accurate transcription?

LILL: I thought it was quite a good and fair transcript. If I had thought it was a completely accurate transcription, I would not have made any changes in it.

CHESSMAN: And I note that you have suggested approximately 1,600 changes or corrections. Now, do you know of any other instance in a reporter's transcript on appeal where that many changes or corrections have been suggested and adopted?

LILL: I know of no instance where a reporter's transcript on appeal has been so checked. I think there are many cases where a reporter, checking his own transcript after having prepared it, would find a number of changes, and, as I have said before, there are a half million words in it.

CHESSMAN: Do you think if you went back over one of your own transcripts you prepared on appeal you would find 1,600 changes or corrections?

LILL: If I read over a half million words, I doubt if I would find 1,600, but I would probably find some.

LILL: I suppose, Mr. Chessman, I would answer that by saying if I had included every variation of a word or a few words which seemed to me to make no difference whatever in the sense, which seemed to me—I realize that is my conclusion; but I was asked to do this as an expert—if I had included every single word, I would have had another volume here of the length of *Gone With the Wind,* probably.

CHESSMAN: And you find, then, that even—now, putting aside your conclusion that there was no difference, if you would have indicated every difference that you found, whether it changed the meaning or not, but where you found differences, in the transcript as compared with Mr. Perry's notes, that you would have had a volume as long as *Gone With the Wind.* Is that correct?

CRAIL: Well, just a moment. He is assuming that the meaning was changed and I don't believe the witness has testified she, at that time, found any difference in the meaning between Mr. Fraser's transcript and Mr. Perry's notes. I object to it for that reason.

CHESSMAN: That is ultimately for the Court to decide and my question was, putting aside her conclusion with respect to the difference.

CRAIL: You asked her a compound question and you slipped that in the first part of the question, probably thinking she wouldn't catch it.

CHESSMAN: You will state definitely there are not six untranscribed outlines at that point?

LILL: I do not find six.

CHESSMAN: Are you presently able to read them?

LILL: I am not, without further study.

THE COURT: What word do they follow in the transcript?

CRAIL: It would be the word "here," on 1039, line 13.

THE COURT: Thank you.

CHESSMAN: To save time, Mr. Crail, I'm willing to stipulate that Mrs. Lill, without exception, when she presently is unable to read these notes will testify that with further study, in her opinion she would be able to read them, because I have noticed that gratuitously every time she has added that and I don't want to keep anything out that perhaps should be in the transcript, so I will stipulate at this point that invariably would be her answer and then we can limit the question, as I have limited in my question, as to whether or not she presently is able to read them.

CRAIL: Well, I don't know that that would be the situation in every instance.

CHESSMAN I would. . . .

LILL: I recognize it as a lengthened "k," quite clearly.

CHESSMAN: How is a lengthened "k" written in shorthand, Mrs. Lill?

LILL: As a lengthened straight line.

CHESSMAN: And you find that this is a lengthened straight line, the ink symbol I am now pointing you to?

LILL: I do.

CHESMAN: And that will be the 1, 2, 3, 4, 5 inked character on line 4 of column 1 or page 71 of the notes; is that correct?

LILL: I do, and, of course, the consonant which precedes it lends somewhat of clarity to the form. The two consonants written as they are, being a recognized symbol for the word "picture."

CHESSMAN: You can read Mr. Perry's shorthand, then, on occasions when you find Mr. Fraser's pencilled shorthand appearing above it or near it; is that correct?

LILL: Yes. It helps greatly in a matter of snap judgment.

CHESSMAN: Well, we haven't been asking you to make a snap judgment, Mrs. Lill. You have had as much time as you wish to take here.

LILL: Compared to the time that I took in making this survey, Mr. Chessman, the term "snap judgment" seems to me to apply.

SMITH: How would you describe the quality of the penmanship in those books?

BURDICK: Well, do you happen to remember whose notes these are you gave me?

SMITH: Those are, I believe, Mr. Fraser's notes, as I recall.

BURDICK: Yes, I don't want to misunderstand. These are practically copperplate.

SMITH: What does the term "copperplate" mean?

BURDICK:[28] It means a writer who has a perfectly steady hand and whose hand was apparently born to hold a pen. That is the only way I can describe it. There are very few living or in the past who are really copperplate writers, and Mr. Fraser is one of them.

SMITH: Now, Mr. Burdick, after examining Mr. Fraser's notes and the transcription, how would you describe Mr. Fraser's approach or his effort?

BURDICK: The last word?

SMITH: Approach or efforts.

BURDICK: Well, it was, I would say, a very conscientious and complete one, burying himself in it for a period of months. That's the only way you can handle a job like that.

DAVIS: All right. Now with reference to these notes, when you read the Perry notebook against the dictated transcription that you were listening to, did you read both the pencil and the ink portions of the Perry notebooks in order to make the comparison, or did you just read the ink or just the pencilled portions?

BURDICK: Of course when I opened that book and saw the pencilled portions I knew exactly why they were there and what it was. I have used that method time and time again, an old expedient, and I didn't take the trouble to look at it except to glance at it from time to time—something like that; but none of that went into—into consideration at all.

DAVIS: Well, did you read both the pencilled and the ink portions when you were reading for the purpose of making a comparison, or did you make it only against the ink portions?

BURDICK: Only against the ink portions, except as I glanced up and saw some of the shorthand casually.

DAVIS: Now would you say that Mr. Perry's shorthand style was reasonable—showed reasonably good penmanship?

BURDICK: For that style, yes.

DAVIS: And would you say that his shorthand style was a readable style?

BURDICK: Not for me. I don't know how it is for Mr. Fraser. Of course he explained that for many years he had been familiar with it, but for one—you see, I started out as a copperplate writer myself, and anyone that writes that style generally, it is so foreign to the way he writes. His is a dashing style.

DAVIS: Of course, being an expert in this case, you can read Mr. Perry's books, can't you?

BURDICK: I couldn't read his books now without going through the study that I went through years ago to learn the systems that I had to work with.

DAVIS: But you were only retained as an expert witness last December of 1955, weren't you?

BURDICK: As an expert witness?

DAVIS: Yes.

BURDICK: No, I wasn't retained as an expert witness until I was told just the other day that I was to come up here and testify.

DAVIS: But you have qualified yourself as an expert on shorthand, and particularly Pitmanic shorthand, and on the shorthand in Mr. Perry's notebooks; isn't that correct?

BURDICK: I don't think I said that I was an expert on Mr. Perry's shorthand. If I did, it was a slip of the tongue. I have learned some of it, of course.

THE COURT:[29] He didn't say that.

DAVIS: But you have purported to give an opinion with reference to this particular writing; isn't that correct?

BURDICK: Certainly.

DAVIS: Well, now, Mr. Burdick, would you do this just before we leave today: Would you take page 107 of this shorthand book—and it is the book that is dated 5/7/48—and would you just read for us the full contents of the page, and would you read it once without the pencilled markings and then read it once more including the pencilled markings?

BURDICK: No, I could not have done that the minute I finished this job. I didn't try to learn his system.

SMITH: Mr. Davis, he had not purported to be able to cold read those notes.

BURDICK: It would take me an hour, at least, and then I might not work it all out.

DAVIS: Well, could you read half the page, then?

BURDICK: Oh, I don't know. Probably not. I can tell you right now there is only an occasional word that I can read right off, you see. You see Mr. Perry's notes, his style that he—his choice of words—his choice of principles that he used over a period of years varies from mine. He might write the same system . . .

THE COURT: May I understand you: You mean that the way that you are able to read those notes is by simultaneously looking at the transcript?

BURDICK: Surely, and knowing what that is supposed to be, and even if it is written in any one of ten different ways—there are lots of words, long words that can be written ten or fifteen different ways, you see.

THE COURT: You can't read the transcript except after long study cold? I mean the notes, you can't read them cold, as it were?

BURDICK: That is correct, Your Honor.

THE COURT: As a matter of fact, sometimes reporters can't read their own notes after a while when they get read cold; is that right?

BURDICK: I have heard that.

CHESSMAN:[30] And when the transcript was completed in final form, and I am referring now to Volumes 4 to 8, inclusive, were you satisfied that this was a verbatim transcription or did you believe it to be less than verbatim?

LEAVY: I feel it was as substantial a transcript as Perry would have been able to get out by himself, as I read it, and I still say that.

CHESSMAN: You believe that this transcript was as good a transcript as Mr. Perry would have produced himself; is that correct?

LEAVY: Substantially, from a lawyer's viewpoint, yes; from a lawyer who participated in the case, as I did.

CHESSMAN: From the prosecutor's viewpoint, you mean, who sent a defendant to the Death Row?[31]

LEAVY: From an attorney on either side of any case.

CHESSMAN: Well, I will ask you, then, do you still maintain that that portion of the transcript referred to by yourself in this affidavit was "a true and correct verbatim question and answer reportorial transcript"?

LEAVY: Yes, as read by me. Keep in mind, I didn't read the shorthand notes.

CHESSMAN: I will do that.

And do you still maintain that the transcript, as submitted to the Court for settlement by yourself, and as approved and settled by the Court, was as good a transcript as Mr. Fraser could have—I mean, as Mr. Perry could have prepared had he lived to do the work?

LEAVY: I feel it was.

CHESSMAN: And had it been brought to your attention at that time that Mr. Fraser had failed to transcribe literally hundreds of Mr. Perry's shorthand symbols, would your testimony be the same?

LEAVY: It would have been the same if Perry had gotten it out. I wouldn't have known the difference.

CHESSMAN: Well, I mean, specifically, if someone had brought to your attention the fact that Mr. Fraser had failed to transcribe literally hundreds of Mr. Perry's shorthand symbols in the portion of the work prepared by Mr. Fraser, would you·still have represented to the Court that this was as good a transcript as Mr. Perry would have prepared himself?

LEAVY: As I read it, yes.

CHESSMAN: And, if an expert appointed by the Court on your own motion, had examined Mr. Fraser's work and made his or her findings known to you, and in those findings, if that expert had shown you where some 1,600 emendations or corrections or changes should, in the expert's opinion, be made, would you still have represented to Judge Fricke that this was as good a transcript as Mr. Perry could have prepared from his own notes?

LEAVY: I would, unless it changed the meaning some place.

CHESSMAN: Well, now, let's get a definition some place of the phrase "change the meaning"?

LEAVY: Well, if a witness took the stand and said you were a person who assaulted him or robbed him, when, as a matter of fact, I knew otherwise, I would say that would change the meaning. That's an example.

CHESSMAN: Well, is it a definition?

LEAVY: Well, that's up to you to decide. That is what I refer to as changing the meaning,[32] and as being an example.

CONCLUDING OBSERVATIONS

Fraser never said his transcription was letter perfect. He said it was the best he could do. The numerous suggestions by Mrs. Lill made it an even better transcript. The objections of Chessman focused on even more weak spots. When Judge Evans went over the transcript, he had the tools to turn out a complete version.

Chessman was in a box. Each technical objection he made to the transcription hurt him. It allowed the court to perfect the transcript. He was working to put himself in the gas chamber. A definite role conflict. He would have had to show that Fraser transcription was so mistake-ridden that it could not be used. He missed doing so by six country miles.

19

Text of the Decision of Judge Evans

Every shorthand reporter who took the stand in this hearing was able to read at least a portion of those [Perry's] notes and the demonstration on the blackboard, by Mrs. Kalin, in the opinion of the Court, corroborated the fact that Mr. Perry's notes could be and were transcribed with substantial accuracy.

Contrary to the claims of the defendant and the testimony of Mrs. Kalin, it is the opinion of this writer that the "perfect" symbols placed upon the blackboard during her testimony were substantially similar in the vast majority of instances to the symbols in Mr. Perry's notes—the only difference being that Mrs. Kalin was drawing "perfect" symbols, taking ample time, while Mr. Perry's notes were written at courtroom speed.

Regarding Mr. Hanna's findings and his testimony, the Court concedes that he certainly had the finest of qualifications to appear as an expert in this case. However, it was obvious that Mr. Hanna either did not have sufficient time to study Mr. Perry's notes or he did not approach his job as objectively as he professed from the witness stand. . . . This Court is of the opinion that had Mr. Hanna had the time to study Mr. Perry's notes, together with that part of the transcript dictated by Mr. Perry, before he began checking Mr. Frazier's [sic] work, he, too would have satisfied himself that the transcript was properly prepared. On the other hand, if he approached his task from the standpoint of an elementary instructor in shorthand to try to find what he could claim as errors or omissions made by Mr. Frazier [sic], his services are of little aid to the Court—particularly when he claims to be a verbatim reporter and then says that no reporters' notes are perfectly accurate. (Mr. Hanna was asked, on cross-examination by the People, "As you examined these notes, were you looking for copybook shorthand?" and replied, "Absolutely not. . . . Why courtroom shorthand is next to impossible in reporting, unless the going is very slow. There is always some departure from the copybook outlines.")

Concerning the charges or insinuations of the defendant that the transcript, herein, was fraudulently prepared. This court has combed the record and has failed to find anything upon which the defendant could base such a claim. . . . The notes of the deceased reporter were examined by several reporters, and after they had expressed opinions that the notes could be transcribed, and after other reporters had been asked if they would undertake the job, and had refused, another disinterested court reporter, Mr. Frazier [sic] was contacted and agreed to do the transcription. His relationship to Mr. Leavy's wife certainly had no part in his having been so employed. In this respect, it is interesting to note that prior to October, 1948 and before anyone interested in the defense of the defendant knew the facts surrounding the employment of a transcriber, and before the transcriptions had been completed, the defendant was advised that his legal advisor was 'elated' that a relative of Mr. Leavy was going to do the transcribing. Certainly, at that time the defense would not have been 'elated' that a transcript could and would be made, and the only logical conclusion is that upon receipt of this information, it was then and there that the defendant's claim of fraud, to be pressed at a later date, was conceived.

Considerable time was consumed during this hearing by the defendant in an attempt to show bias and prejudice on the part of Judge Fricke and Mr. Leavy. The record is completely void of any evidence to show that Judge Fricke had any feeling of bias or prejudice against the defendant prior to or during the trial of his case. At the time Judge Fricke ruled on defendant's motion for a new trial, and when he pronounced judgment upon the defendant, it is a certainty that he then believed that the evidence produced during the trial was sufficient to justify the jury's verdict or he would have granted the defendant a new trial. His public expressions of his belief in the defendant's guilt came after he had completed the defendant's case and after he had heard the evidence for and against the defendant, and indicated only that he was exercising the right to state his opinion just as any other person might do.

As regards Mr. Leavy, this Court is at a loss as to the reason for questioning him relative to his belief, prior to the time of trial, that the defendant was guilty. In the opinion of this Court, a district attorney who prosecuted a man whom he did not believe was guilty prior to the commencement of such prosecution would verge very closely upon a violation of his oath of office.

As regards the claim by the defendant that during the time the jury was deliberating and when they returned to the courtroom for further instructions, Judge Fricke instructed them that the defendant was one of the worst criminals he had had in his court, and that the jury should bring in the death penalty, this is purely a figment of the defendant's imagination which was conceived several years after the time of his trial, and it is the opinion of this Court that many of the other claimed omissions and errors are of a similar nature.

Most of the defendant's claims of fraud and of bias and prejudice can be attributed to the fact that at all times during, for some time after his trial, he refused to be represented by counsel and he could never be made to understand that, as a prisoner first charged with, and then convicted of, very serious crimes, he was not and could not be accorded the same freedom of movement and the same access to conveniences that would be accorded an attorney representing a defendant, or a deputy district attorney.

As to the claimed disability of Mr. Frazier [sic] due to his use of intoxicants, everyone will concede that he had at times, over quite a number of years, been in trouble due to his drinking.

However, after observing him on the witness stand over a period of ten days and considering all of the evidence at this hearing, this Court concludes that his work on this transcript was not affected in any way by his use of alcohol. He testified that he had not had a drink for a considerable period of time prior to commencing work on the transcript on appeal, nor did he take a drink during the time he was doing this work. The only real evidence that this testimony is in conflict with, is that of the two witnesses who operated a liquor store in the vicinity of Mr. Frazier's [sic] home. In this respect, it is interesting to note that the gist of the testimony of these two women was that Mr. Frazier [sic] was intoxicated 97 percent of the time they knew him: that they sold him from one to five pints of liquor a day, but that they never sold him liquor when he was intoxicated. This type of evidence speaks for itself and no further comment is necessary.

It is also of interest that throughout this entire hearing, the only opinions expressed on the ability of both Mr. Frazier [sic] and Mr. Perry were that they were both excellent court reporters. The fact that Mr. Frazier [sic] was arrested once during the time he was preparing the transcript in augmentation of the record on appeal in no way changes the conclusion heretofore mentioned.

While the changes to be made as listed in Exhibit A attached hereto are many in number, [in fact, they were 2,000 in number], a study of these changes makes it very clear that, considering them either individually or collectively, they in no way change the substance and nature of either the People's case or the defendant's defense.

Notes

[1]Deputy District Attorney, Los Angeles County.

[2]Superior Court, Los Angeles County.

[3]Later testimony indicated that friendship and collaboration occurred again on less formal basis when both were Superior Court employees in Los Angeles during the 1930s.

[4]By the time of this hearing, 1957, machine writing had supplanted handwriting for the most part in courtroom reporting.

[5]On cross-examination, Chessman, defending himself, delves into the appointment of Fraser to translate the notes of Perry.

[6]Paul M. Posner, an attorney hired by Chessman to assist him during this hearing.

[7]To conform to evidentiary rules, X was subsituted for Fraser in the original. The hypothetical was used so that a psychiatrist could render an opinion as to the condition of a person he had not examined. Only the facts supporting the hypothesis are important for our purposes.

[8]Notice the small number of convictions and lightness of punishment as compared to the number of arrests. Fraser's courtroom position may be the explanation for this.

[9]Helen Arthur, later Helen Arthur Fraser, typed many transcript notes dictated by Fraser. Thus her sobriety is important also.

[10]Mrs. Eleanor Shure is the daughter of the proprietor of a liquor store patronized by Fraser around the time he was preparing the Chessman transcript.

[11]A loaded question. Selling liquor to an intoxicated person could cause loss of liquor license and is a crime. Chessman should have objected to it as tending to cause the witness to incriminate herself.

[12]Within a month, Fricke would be dead of cancer, but the disease had not yet dulled his quick wits.

[13]Statement made by Mr. Crail during final argument.

[14]Reference to January 1956 *habeas corpus* hearing in San Francisco before Federal District Court Judge Louis E. Goodman.

[15]Chessman actually is referring to the last five volumes. Volume 1 to 3 had been transcribed by Perry before his death. Volumes 4 to 8 were transcribed by Fraser.

[16]Leavy contradicts Fraser. He claims he sent Fraser to talk with the two police witnesses. The point doesn't seem crucial.

[17]Bessie Lill was a seventy-four year old retired courtroom reporter. Her expert testimony was most damaging to Chessman. She had a great feel for courtroom conditions. Chessman was unable to refute her assertions concerning continuity of the Perry notes.

[18]Arlo Smith was Deputy Attorney General for the State of California.

[19]Paul Burdick was a long-time Los Angeles County Superior Courtroom reporter and the author of the standard Japanese texts on shorthand. All of his testimony occured at the earlier 1956 Federal District Court *habeas corpus* hearing in San Francisco, not at the 1957 California Superior Court hearing presently under consideration. Mr. Burdick was excused from testifying again because he had become senile in the interim. California law did not, then, permit testimony from an earlier hearing to be read into a later hearing when senility was the reason for the failure of production of the evidence at the second hearing. This material, consequently, never was considered by Judge Evans in arriving at his decision in the 1957 hearing under consideration. Burdick's testimony is included herein to round out the picture.

[20]George T. Davis, famous San Fransisco attorney, represented Chessman in the January 1956 *habeas corpus* petition hearing. This section is from his forceful cross-examination of Burdick.

[21]From here on testimony is again from the 1957-1958 California Superior Court hearing in Los Angeles.

[22]Frank Hanna was a prestigious shorthand expert with more than fifty years experience at the time of the Chessman hearing. He had been the stenographer for the famous William Jennings Bryan "Cross of Gold" speech and had conducted a Success Shorthand School in New York City. Chessman forces had approached him concerning the Perry notes.

[23]Volume 4 is the first volume that Fraser transcribed. Perry had transcribed the first three volumes himself.

[24]J. Miller Leavy was prosecuting the Ewing L. Scott murder case during the pendency of this 1957 hearing. Other than as a witness, his appearances in the *Chessman* hearing were few and far between.

[25]Mollie Kalin was a Los Angeles housewife who volunteered to assist Chessman during this hearing. Before her marriage she had spent twenty years as a stenographer. The prosecution was quick to observe that none of this had been in courtroom stenography.

[26]This could explain the fact that neither Fraser nor Leavy thought to mention their family relationship to Judge Fricke.

[27]This statement is totally at variance with my dealings with Mr. Leavy. Mr. Leavy, at the age of sixty-eight, has the most extraordinary memory of names, facts, statutes, and cases that I have ever encountered.

[28]Again, the Burdick testimony was at the San Francisco hearing in 1956 and was not part of the 1957 California Superior Court hearing and had no influence upon the 1957 decision.

[29]The judge referred to at this point is Judge Goodman, not Judge Evans.

[30]A return to the testimony in the California Superior Court.

[31]Clearly there is still no love lost between Chessman and Leavy.

[32]Leavy well illustrates the fatal flaw in Chessman's argument. He never could demonstrate any major omissions or changes in meaning.

Chronology*

May 27, 1921. Carol Whittier Chessman born, St. Joseph, Michigan. (Later changed spelling of first name to Caryl.)

November 1921. Chessman family moves to Glendale, California.

July 15, 1937. Sentenced to Preston Industrial School for vehicle theft and burglary.

April 1938. Released from Preston.

May 6, 1938. Arrested in Glendale for vehicle theft and forgery.

May 7, 1938. Recommitted to Preston.

June 1939. Paroled for good behavior from Preston.

October 13, 1939. Arrested for car theft; sentenced to Los Angeles County Jail and assigned to road camp.

June 30, 1940. Paroled from county jail.

April 28, 1941. Convicted of robbery and assault with a deadly weapon.

May 7, 1941. Sentenced to San Quentin Prison for auto theft, assaulting a police officer and robbery.

May 27, 1943. Transferred to Chino Correctional Institution.

October 1943. Escaped from Chino.

November 1943. Arrested in Glendale.

December 21, 1943. Convicted of robbery.

---

*This chronology is a modified version of that in William M. Kuntsler, *Beyond A Reasonable Doubt? The Original Trial of Caryl Chessman* (New York: William Morrow and Co., 1961) pp. 291-98.

January 18, 1944. Sentenced to five years to life at San Quentin on recommitment.

August 6, 1945. Sent to maximum security Folsom State Prison.

December 8, 1947. Paroled from Folsom.

January 3, 1948. Holdup at Hoelscher's Pasadena haberdashery.

January 13, 1948. Rose K. Howell's Ford coupe stolen in Pasadena.

January 17, 1948. Attempted burglary of Tarro home in Glendale.

January 18, 1948. 4:35 A.M. robbery of Dr. Thomas Bartle near Malibu Beach.

January 18, 1948. Floyd E. Ballew and Elaine Bushaw robbed near Rose Bowl around 7:30 P.M.

January 19, 1948. Jarnigan Lea and Regina Johnson robbed in Flintridge Hills; Regina Johnson sexually molested.

January 20, 1948. Gerald Stone and Esther Panasuk robbery on Mulholland Drive.

January 22, 1948. Kidnapping and sexual molestation of Mary Alice Meza.

January 23, 1948. Armed robbery at Town Clothiers, Redondo Beach.

January 23, 1948. Chessman and David H. Knowles arrested after a five mile chase down Vermont Avenue, Los Angeles.

January 26, 1948. Chessman transferred to Los Angeles County Jail.

February 18, 1948. Original informations filed in Los Angeles Superior Court.

February 20, 1948. Arraigned with Knowles. Morris Lavine appears as legal counsel for Chessman.

February 27, 1948. Amended informations filed in Los Angeles Superior Court.

March 5, 1948. Arraigned on amended informations. V.L. Ferguson represented Chessman.

March 9, 1948. Chessman fired Ferguson. Time to plead extended to March 12.

March 12, 1948. Public Defender relieved. Not guilty pleas entered.

March 18, 1948. Refuses services of Deputy Public Defender Al Matthews.

March - June, 1948. Visited in jail by Attorney William Roy Ives.

April 26, 1948. Motion granted to be tried separately from Knowles.

April 29, 1948. Chessman refused services of public defender as legal counsel; offer of Al Mattnews to act as his legal advisor accepted next day.

April 30, 1948. Eighteen count felony trial, *People* v. *Chessman,* begins in Department 43, Los Angeles County Superior Court; Hon. Charles W. Fricke, presiding; Chessman defends self.

May 3, 1948. Jury of eleven women and one man impaneled.

May 21, 1948. Found guilty on seventeen counts, including two 209 kidnapping charges for which the jury decides upon death as the penalty.

June 23, 1948. Court Reporter Ernest W. Perry dies after converting one-third of his Chessman trial shorthand notes into English. The rest of the record remains in its original, shorthand state.

June 25, 1948. Judge Fricke passes the official sentence of death and refuses Chessman's motion for a new trial because of the death of the court reporter.

July 2, 1948. Chessman files Notice of Appeal with Clerk, Los Angeles County Superior Court.

July - August 1948. Visited in San Quentin Death Row by Sacramento attorney Rosalie S. Asher at request of Al Matthews.

July 1948. Perry notes turned over to Stanley Fraser who will attempt to read and transcribe them.

September 7, 1948. Fraser indicates willingness to attempt task and is employed for this purpose by Los Angeles County Board of Supervisors.

October 16, 1948. Los Angeles County Superior Court Reporters, Association Executive Committee protests by letter to County Supervisors that the Perry notes are unreadable.

November 1, 1948. Chessman files petition for writ of prohibition with California Supreme Court, attacking attempts to prepare transcript.

November 22, 1948. California Supreme Court denies petition for writ of prohibition.

February 1949. Fraser sends rough draft of completed transcript to Judge Fricke.

April 11, 1949. Fraser certifies portion of transcript he prepared; copy sent to Chessman at San Quentin.

May 10, 1949. Chessman files motion with Clerk, Los Angeles County Superior Court attacking transcript.

June 3, 1949. Judge Fricke certifies transcript as the accurate trial record. Fricke held three day hearing on matter at which Chessman was not permitted to appear and was not represented by attorney.

June 10, 1949. The trial transcript in the Chessman case, which Fricke had certified as being accurate over the objections of Chessman, is sent to the California Supreme Court for use in deciding Chessman's appeal.

June 15, 1949. The California Supreme Court Clerk writes Chessman at San Quentin to ask if he will hire an attorney for the appeal, or should one be provided for him.

June 30, 1949. Chessman, acting for himself, files by mail with the California Supreme Court a motion to "impeach, correct, and certify the transcript."

August 15, 1949. Having received no answer to his first letter, the California Supreme Court Clerk writes Chessman a letter identical to that of June 15.

August 18, 1949. At the direction of the California Supreme Court, Fricke holds a hearing to deal with the Chessman motion of June 30, 1949. Chessman neither present nor represented at this hearing. Fricke again finds the transcript accurate for the purpose of the appeal before the California Supreme Court.

September 21, 1949. Chessman hires Rosalie Asher as his attorney for the appeal before the California Supreme Court.

September 23, 1949. Chessman dismisses Miss Asher and again chooses to represent himself. In an attempt to block the California Supreme Court from holding the appeal hearing where the death penalty might be confirmed, he files a motion for writ of *habeas corpus* in the United States District Court. (The intent is to have the court declare he is being held illegally. A man is entitled by right to an appeal in a death case. If the State can't give it to him, they must retry him.)

March 17, 1950. United States District Court Judge Louis E. Goodman denies Chessman's application for a writ of *habeas corpus*. This permits the appeal hearing by California Supreme Court (unless a higher court overrules Goodman or California Supreme Court) and overrules Fricke and decides transcript is not accurate enough to be used as the basis of an appeal.

May 12, 1950. Chessman files a petition with California Supreme Court seeking a writ of *habeas corpus* on grounds transcript is not accurate enough for an appeal. The Court must deal with this objection before hearing the appeal.

May 19, 1950. California Supreme Court denies the application for a *habeas corpus* writ that would have brought Chessman a new trial. Simultaneously, the Court dismisses Chessman's appeal from Fricke's certifications of the transcript (on June 10 and August 18, 1949), but orders two additions to the transcript. It appears that the way is clear to actual consideration of the appeal but Chessman immediately files a motion asking reconsideration of the decision.

June 12, 1950. California Supreme Court refuses to review its decision of May 19, 1950. Again it denies Chessman *habeas corpus* which would have resulted in a new trial. Chessman tries United States Supreme Court.

October 9, 1950. United States Supreme Court refuses to intervene.

December 4, 1950. United States District Court refuses to order a new trial. *Habeas corpus* denied.

February 27, 1951. At Chessman's request, the next highest federal court, United States Court of Appeals, reviews the December 4, 1950 decision, and affirms it. Chessman immediately appeals this decision to United States Supreme Court.

May 14, 1951. United States Supreme Court again refuses to consider the case. Now that all state and Federal courts have refused to order a new trial on the grounds the trial transcript was inadequate, California Supreme Court finally is able to rule on Chessman's appeal.

December 18, 1951. California Supreme Court denies Chessman's appeal. (This is an official declaration that he was properly convicted and sentenced to death.) Chessman immediately files for a rehearing on the appeal and also again seeks a new trial via *habeas corpus* on the grounds the trial transcript is defective.

December 18, 1951. Judge Fricke sets March 28, 1952 as date for Chessman execution.

January 15, 1952. California Supreme Court refuses to review its December 18, 1951 decision. The motion for a writ of *habeas corpus* is denied.

February 29, 1952. Judge Jesse W. Carter postpones the execution while United States Supreme Court considers whether to honor Chessman's request that they review California Supreme Court decisions of December 18, 1951 and January 15, 1952. This is Chessman's first stay of execution.

March 7. 1952. Judge Fricke orders San Quentin authorities to give Chessman certain privileges.

March 31, 1952. United States Supreme Court refuses to consider the case.

April 28, 1952. Chessman files immediately for rehearing. On this date, United States Supreme Court refuses the request. (In theory, this is the end. Both his *habeas corpus* writ application and his conviction appeal have gone to the highest court in the land without success.) Chessman tries Judge Goodman again on the *habeas corpus* writ.

June 9, 1952. Goodman refuses the writ application. Execution set for June 27, 1952.

June 23, 1952. Judge Albert Lee Stephens of United States District Court grants a stay of execution so that Chessman can appeal the June 9 decision of Goodman to United States Court of Appeals. This is the second stay of execution.

May 28, 1953. Nearly twelve months later, United States Court of Appeals affirms the June 9, 1952, decision of Goodman. Chessman moves to challenge this decision in United States Supreme Court.

December 14, 1953. United States Supreme Court refuses to hear the case. Chessman asks for rehearing.

February 1, 1954. Rehearing refused by United States Supreme Court. Execution scheduled for May 14, 1954.

May 4, 1954. Chessman retains Berwyn A. Rice as legal counsel.

May 13, 1954. Rice asks the Superior Court in the county in which San Quentin is located to grant Chessman a writ of *habeas corpus* so a new trial can occur.

May 13, 1954. Rice finds Judge Carter camping in mountains. The judge grants Chessman a stay of execution while Rice's *habeas corpus* writ application is being considered. This is third stay of execution.

May 24, 1954. The application for a writ of *habeas corpus* is refused by Superior Court in San Quentin's home county. An application for the same writ is filed with the California Supreme Court.

June 1954. Prentice-Hall publishes Chessman's autobiography. (It becomes an inter-national best seller, appearing in eighteen languages. Entitles *Cell 2455, Death Row,* it was written surreptitiously and smuggled out of the prison. Later, Chessman writes three other books under similar conditions.)

July 21, 1954. California Supreme Court again refuses the application for a writ of *habeas corpus.* Execution is set for July 30, 1954.

July 28, 1954. Judge Carter grants Chessman his fourth stay of execution so that he again may petition United States Supreme Court. Attorney General for the State of California asks California Supreme Court to cancel the stay of execution granted by Carter.

August 19, 1954. California Supreme Court refuses to set aside the stay of execution.

October 25, 1954. United States Supreme Court refuses to consider the matter, but for the first time specifically allows Chessman to file a writ of *habeas corpus* in the proper Unites States District Court. Chessman goes right back to Judge Goodman with the claim the trial transcript was inadequate.

January 4, 1955. Goodman dismisses the writ of *habeas corpus.* Execution set for January 14, 1955.

January 11, 1955. United States Court of Appeals Chief Judge William Denman grants Chessman his fifth stay of execution so that he can appeal Goodman's decision of January 4.

February 1, 1955. California Supreme Court cancels privileges Chessman had been given for his defense.

April 7, 1955. United States Court of Appeals affirms Goodman's writ denial. Chessman requests rehearing.

May 6, 1955. Rehearing denied. Execution set for July 15, 1955.

July 5, 1955. United States Supreme Court Justice Tom Clark grants Chessman his sixth execution stay so he can again request United States Supreme Court to hear the case.

October 17, 1955. United States Supreme Court refuses to consider the case, but orders Goodman to hold a hearing as to whether a writ of *habeas corpus* should issue because of fraud in transcript preparation.

January 16-25, 1956. Hearing before Goodman in United States District Court, San Francisco. Chessman represents himself, assisted by Attorney George T. Davis.

January 31, 1956. Goodman finds no fraud in transcript preparation; denies writ. Chessman appeals ruling to United States Court of Appeals.

October 18, 1956. Nine months later, United States Court of Appeals rules that Goodman was correct. Chessman returns to United States Supreme Court and asks it to consider the matter.

April 8, 1957. United States Supreme Court agrees to consider the Chessman case.

June 10, 1957. United States Supreme Court rules Fricke was in error when he refused Chessman permission to be present at the transcript certification hearings of June 3 and August 18, 1949. The case is returned to this point. Fricke is ordered to hold another transcript certification hearing with Chessman present. (If the transcript again is certified, it will be necessary for the California Supreme Court to rehear Chessman's official appeal.)

November 25, 1957 to February 14, 1958. Transcript certification hearing is held in Los Angeles before Superior Court Judge Walter R. Evans, replacing Fricke who is in ill health. Chessman represents himself, assisted by Attorney Paul Posner.

February 28, 1958. Evans approves transcript with corrections. Chessman files for new hearing before Goodman.

April 2, 1958. Goodman refuses to reconsider matter.

May 1, 1958. Evans certifies transcript and orders copy sent to Chessman at San Quentin, which is done on May 13.

June 19, 1958. Corrected transcript filed with California Supreme Court for use in judging the appeal of Chessman from his conviction and sentence.

July 2, 1958. Chessman files an appeal with California Supreme Court objecting to Evans' transcript certification decision in general, and to ninety of the corrections he ordered in particular.

October 2, 1958. California Supreme Court orders Evans to hold further hearings concerning the ninety specific objections. The Court puts off to a later date decision on whether Evans was correct in certifying the transcript. Thus the appeal also is postponed.

October - November 1958. Evans holds a hearing on the ninety corrections.

December 10, 1958. Before receiving the decision of Evans, California Supreme Court decides the question it put off earlier and affirms Evans' transcript certification decision of February 28, 1958. Coast is clear to consider Chessman's appeal once Evans deals with the ninety corrections.

December 12, 1958. Evans hands down his decision on the ninety corrections and recertifies the whole transcript. Chessman attempts to have United States Supreme Court declare the whole California certification procedure illegal.

April 26, 1959. United States Supreme Court refuses to consider Chessman's motion. The California Supreme Court continues to work on Chessman's appeal to his trial conviction and sentence.

July 7, 1959. California Supreme Court affirms Chessman's conviction and upholds the death sentence.

August 10, 1959. Execution date set for October 24, 1959.

October 15, 1959. California Governor Edmund G. Brown hears a plea to commute Chessman's sentence to life in prison without the possibility of parole.

October 19, 1959. Governor refuses to grant clemency.

October 21, 1959. United States Supreme Court Justice William O. Douglas grants Chessman his seventh stay of execution so that he can again request United States Supreme Court consider the case.

December 14, 1959. United States Supreme Court refuses to consider the case. Chessman requests reconsideration.

January 11, 1960. United States Supreme Court refuses to reconsider. Execution set for February 19, 1960.

January 29, 1960. Judge Goodman of United States District Court refuses to consider yet another application by Chessman for a writ of *habeas corpus.* Chessman appeals to the United States Court of Appeals.

February 8, 1960. United States Court of Appeals Judge Richard H. Chambers affirms the January 29 decision of Goodman.

February 15, 1960. United States Court of Appeals refuses Chessman motion for a stay of execution.

February 17, 1960. United States Supreme Court denies Chessman motion to declare the California transcript certification procedure illegal.

February 18, 1960. California Supreme Court refuses to recommend clemency to Governor Brown.

February 18, 1960. Brown grants Chessman a sixty-day stay of execution and recommends abolition of death penalty to California Legislature. Eighth execution stay.

March 2, 1960. Execution set for May 2, 1960

March 9, 1960. California Supreme Court refuses to annul death warrant.

March 10, 1960. California State Senate Judiciary Committee kills death penalty abolition bill.

April 25, 1960. Justice Douglas refuses to grant stay of execution.

April 29, 1960. California Supreme Court again refuses to recommend clemency to Brown.

May 2, 1960. At 9:05 A.M. California Supreme Court refuses to grant *habeas corpus;* at 10:03 A.M., Judge Goodman agrees to sixty minute stay of execution to read new arguments of attorneys Davis and Asher. This would have been ninth stay of execution, but it would have been futile because Justice Douglas with final authority denied same motion simultaneously in Washington.

May 2, 1960. At 10:03 A.M., after twelve years on Death Row, the longest in United States history, Caryl Chessman is gassed to death.

Bibliography

Books

de Beaumont, Jolie and Francois de Montford. *Le Mystère Chessman.* Paris: Pressed de la Cité, 1960.

Berro, Huertas. *La Pena de Muerte.* Montevideo, Uruguay: Private Edition, 1961.

Camerero, Julio. *Yo hable Con Chessman.* Madrid: Pueblo, 1960.

Castilio, Ernesto Rodan. *Chessman, El Chivo Expiato.* Mexico City: Editorial Artulguy, 1960.

Camboid, Giselle. *Chessman i.e. Dozo Años A Espera de Morte.* Rio de Janeiro: Editorial Veechi, 1960.

Chessman, Caryl. *Cell 2455, Death Row.* New York: Prentice-Hall, 1954. (An expanded edition was published in 1960).

———. *The Face of Justice.* Englewood Cliffs, N.J.: Prentice-Hall, 1957.

———. *Fils de la Haine,* trans. Louis Chantemele (French version of Chessman's novel, *The Kid Was a Killer*). Paris: *Presses Pocket, 1963.*

———. *Trial by Ordeal.* Englewood Cliffs, N.J.: Prentice-Hall, 1955.

Kunstler, William. *Beyond a Reasonable Doubt? The Original Trial of Caryl Chessman.* New York: William Morrow Co., 1961.

La Pierre, Dominique. *Chessman M'a Dit.* Paris: Del Dica Co., 1960.

Machlin, Milton and William Read Woodfield. *Ninth Life.* New York: G. P. Putnam's Sons, 1961.

Mirodan, Alexander. *In Chessmans Todeszille* (play focussing on capital punishment). Vienna: Verlag Co., 1966.

Morgan, Pedro. *Canto A Un Condemno A Muerte* (poems). Santiago, Chile: Editorial Universitaria, 1960.

Sillonville, Ollivia. *Derrière Les Manchettes.* Montreal: Librairie de Beauche Man, 1966.

Walker, Bill, in collaboration with J. Miller Leavy. *The True Story of the Barbara Graham Case.* Los Angeles: Ace Books, 1961.

Williams, Brad. *Due Process: The Fabulous Story of George T. Davis and His Thirty-Year Battle Against Capital Punishment.* New York: William Morrow Co., 1960.

Articles, Documents, and Notes

Ancel, Marc. "L'Execution de Caryle Chessman et la Peine de Mort," *Revue de Science Criminal et de Droit Penal Criminal,* 1960, 447.

Chessman, Caryl. "A Letter from Death Row," *Psychology Today,* February 1969, 29.

Chessman v Teets. Comments on this case in: *American Bar Association Journal,* XLIII (1957): 735; *Notre Dame Lawyer,* XXXII (1957): 522; *Pennsylvania Law Review,* CV (1957): 1091; *West Virginia,* LX (1957): 117.

"Death or Disability of Court Reporter Before Transcription or Completion of Notes or Record as Ground for New Trial or Reversal," *American Law Reports,* 2d, XIX (as amended, 1970): 1098-1108. Rochester, N.Y.: Lawyers' Cooperative Publishing Co., 1970.

Furman v. Georgia. United States Law Week, XL (1972): 4921.

Gurney, Winifred. "The Case of Eleven 55 Notebooks," *Transcript,* XVII (1959): 29.

Manak, James P. "Case Commentaries and Briefs," *Prosecutor: Journal of the National District Attorneys Association,* VII, VIII (1970-1972).

Note. "Post-Conviction Remedies in California Death Cases," *Stanford Law Review,* XI (1958): 94.

Note. "The Caryl Chessman Case: A Legal Analysis," *Minnesota Law Review,* XLIV (1951): 941.

Note. "Will This Convicted Killer Become Another Chessman?" Editorial in the official journal of the New York State Shorthand Reporters Association, Transcript, XVIII (1960): 3.

Parker, Frank J., S.J. "Aspects of Merger in the Law of Kidnapping," *Cornell Law Review,* LV (1970): 527.

San Quentin Prison, Warden's Office. Death Book; Register.

Book Reviews

Reviews of Caryl Chessman's *Trial by Ordeal* appered in: *Stanford Law Review*, VIII (1956): 304; *American Bar Association Journal*, XLII (1956): 854; *Boston University Law Review*, XXXVI (1956): 326; *Chicago-Kent Law Review*, XXXIII (1955): 384; *Dickinson Law Review*, LX (1955): 100; *Hastings Law Journal*, VII (1956): 234; *New York University Law Review*, XXX, 1466; *Oregon Law Review*, XXXV (1955): 58; *Southern California Law Review*, XXIX (1955): 132; *Texas Law Review*, XXXIV (1956): 675; *Detroit Law Journal*, XXXIII (1955): 88; *Pittsburg Law Journal*, XVII (1956): 317.

Wall, Patrick. Book review: *Beyond a Reasonable Doubt?* by William M. Kuntsler, and *Ninth Life* by Milton Machlin and William Read Woodfield, *Minnesota Law Review*, XL (1962): 804.

Magazine Articles on Chessman

America, June 19, 1954; March 5, 1960; May 7, 1960.

Christian Century, March 16, 1960.

Commonweal, March 4, 1960; March 18, 1960.

Coronet, August 1960.

Good Housekeeping, August 1960.

Life, February 29, 1960; May 9, 1960.

Nation, October 17, 1959; December 26, 1959; February 20, 1960; March 12, 1960; March 26, 1960; April 11, 1960; April 25, 1960; May 14, 1960; May 21, 1960.

Newsweek, February 22, 1954; May 3, 1954; May 24, 1954; August 2, 1954; November 2, 1959; February 29, 1960; March 21, 1960; May 2, 1960; May 9, 1960.

New Republic, March 7, 1960; March 21, 1960; April 25, 1960.

New York Sunday News, November 24, 1957.

Reporter, April 19, 1960; May 26, 1960.

Saturday Review, October 5, 1957; April 23, 1960; May 14, 1960; August 6, 1961.

Time, February 29, 1960; March 21, 1960.

U.S. News and World Report, February 29, 1960; March 14, 1960; May 16, 1960.

Related Material

Books

Alexander, M. E. *Jail Administration.* Springfield, Ill.: Charles C. Thomas Co., 1957.

American Bar Association, Section of Judicial Administration. *The Improvement of the Administration of Justice.* Chicago: American Bar Association, 1971

Bedau, H. A. *The Death Penalty in America.* Chicago: Aldine Publishing Co., 1968.

Belli, Melvin M. *Blood Money.* New York: Grosset and Dunlap, 1956.

Brancale, Ralph and Arthur Ellis. *Psychology of Sex Offenders.* Springfield, Ill.: Charles C. Thomas Co., 1956.

Cambridge Department of Criminal Science. *Sexual Offenses.* New York: Saint Martin's Press, 1957.

Carlin, Jerome E. *Lawyers' Ethics.* New York: Russell Sage Foundation, 1966.

Davis, Bernice Freeman with Al Hirschberg. *The Desperate and the Damned.* New York: Thomas Y. Crowell Co., 1961.

De River, Joseph Paul, M.D. *The Sexual Criminal: A Psychoanalytical Study.* Springfield, Ill.: Charles C. Thomas Co., 1956.

_____. *Crime and the Sexual Psychopath.* Springfield, Ill.: Charles C. Thomas Co., 1958.

Douglas, William O. *We the Judges.* Garden City, N. Y.: Doubleday Co., 1956.

Drzazga, John. *Sex Crimes and Their Legal Aspects.* Springfield, Ill.: Charles C. Thomas Co., 1960.

Duffy, Clinton T., as told to Dean Jennings. *San Quentin Story.* Garden City, N. Y.: Doubleday Co., 1950.

_____, with Al Hirschberg. *88 Men and 2 Women.* Garden City, New York: Doubleday Co., 1962.

East, William. *Society and the Criminal.* Springfield, Ill.: Charles C. Thomas Co., 1951.

Fricke, Charles W. *California Criminal Procedure,* 4th ed. Los Angeles: O. W. Smith Co., 1955.

_____. *California Peace Officers Manual,* 9th ed. Los Angeles: O. W. Smith Co., 1955.

_____. *California Criminal Law,* 6th ed. Los Angeles: O. W. Smith Co., 1956.

_____. *California Criminal Evidence,* 4th ed. Los Angeles: O. W. Smith Co., 1957.

_____. *Planning and Trying Cases,* revised ed. Saint Paul, Minnesota: West Publishing Co., 1959.

_____. *Sentence and Probation: The Imposition of Penalties Upon Convicted Criminals.* Los Angeles: Legal Book Co., 1960.

_____. *5000 Criminal Definitions, Terms and Phrases,* 5th ed. Los Angeles: Legal Book Co., 1968.

Gillette, Paul J. *The Lopinson Case.* Los Angeles: Holloway House Publishing Co., 1967.

Glueck, Sheldon. *Criminal Law and Its Enforcement.* Saint Paul, Minn.: West Publishing Co., 1951.

Grunhut, Max, Rudolf Sieverts, and Jacob M. Van Bemmelen. *Sexual Crime Today.* The Hague: Martinus Nijhoff, 1960.

Huie, William Bradford. *The Execution of Private Slovik.* Boston: Little, Brown and Co., 1954.

Inbau, Fred E. *Lie Detection and Criminal Investigation,* Chicago: Will and Wilk Co., 1953.

Jackson, George. *Soledad Brother.* London: Penguin Books, 1971.

Kalven, Harry, Jr., and Hans Zeisel. *The American Jury.* Boston: Little, Brown and Co., 1966.

Kinsey, Alfred C., and Waidell B. Pomeroy, and Clyde C. Martin. *Sexual Behavior in the Human Male.* Philadelphia: W.D. Saunders Co., 1948.

Lamott, Kenneth. *Chronicles of San Quentin.* New York: David McKay Co., 1961.

LeFave, Wayne R. *Arrest: The Decision to Take a Suspect into Custody.* Boston: Little, Brown and Co., 1965.

Lefkowitz, Bernard, and Kenneth G. Gross. *The Victims.* New York: G. P. Putnam's Sons, 1970.

Leiberman, Charles, ed. *Directory of American Judges.* Chicago: American Directories, 1955.

Leibert, Julius A., with Emily Kingsbery. *Behind Bars.* Garden City, N. Y.: Doubleday Co., 1965.

Lewis, Elmer, ed. *Crime, Kidnapping and Prison Laws.* Washington: U.S. Government Printing Office, 1951.

Llewellyn, Carl. *The Common Law Tradition: Deciding Appeals.* Boston: Little, Brown and Co., 1960.

McClellan, Grant. *Capital Punishment.* New York: Wilson Co., 1961.

McDonald, John M., M.D. *Rape.* Springfield, Ill.: Charles C. Thomas Co., 1971.

Mersky, Roy M., and J. Myron Jacobstein. *Ten Year Index to Periodical Articles Relating to Law.* Dobbs Ferry, N. Y.: Blanville Publications, Inc., 1970.

Orfield, Lester, *Criminal Appeals in America.* Boston: Little, Brown and Co., 1939.

————. *Criminal Procedure from Arrest to Appeal.* New York: New York University Press, 1947.

————. *Criminal Procedure Under the Federal Rules.* Rochester, New York: Lawyers Cooperative Publishing Co., 1967.

Parker, Frank J., S.J. *The Law and the Urban Poor.* Maryknoll, N.Y.: Orbis Books, 1973.

Rawson, Tabor. *I Want to Live.* New York: Signet Books, 1958.

Reinhardt, James M. *Sex Perversion and Sex Crimes.* Springfield, Ill.: Charles C. Thomas Co., 1957.

Scudder, Kenyon J. *Prisoners Are People.* Garden City, N. Y.: Doubleday Co., 1952.

Sjowal, Maj, and Per Wahloo. *Roseanna.* New York: Random House, 1967.

Traver, Robert. *Anatomy of a Murder.* New York: Saint Martin's Press, 1958.

Villon, Francois. *Oeuvres.* Paris: Editions Gurnier Frères, 1970.

Williams, Eugene D. et al. *Los Angeles Murders.* New York: Duell, Sloan and Pearce, 1947.

Zeisel, Hans, Harry Kalven, Jr., and Bernard Buchholz. *Delay in the Court,* Boston: Little, Brown and Co., 1959.

Articles, Comments, Notes

Abramowitz, Elkan, and David Paget. "Executive Clemency," *New York University Law Review,* XXXIX (1964): 136.

American Bar Association Project on Standards of Criminal Justice, "The Judge's Role in Dealing with Trial Disruptions," Chicago: American Bar Association, 1971.

Ashman, Allan. "Capital Punishment Banned in California," *American Bar Association Journal,* LVIII (1972): 402.

Baker, Richard C. "Federal Control of State Criminal Justice," *Missouri Law Review,* XXII (1957): 109.

Bedau, H.A. "The Courts, the Constitution and Capital Punishment," *Utah Law Review,* 1968, 201.

Boyko, Edgar Paul. "The Case Against Electronic Court Reporting," *American Bar Association Journal,* LVI (1971): 1008.

California Legislature Judiciary Committee, Sub-Committee on Capital Punishment. "Report on Problems of the Death Penalty and Its Administration in California," *California Assembly Journal App,* III, vol. 21, no. 1 (1957).

Cohen, J. "Opinion of the Court in the Kulik Case," *Pennsylvania Shorthand Reporters Association Journai,* XXIV (1966): 28.

Comment. "The Death Penalty Cases," *California Law Review,* LVI (1968): 1268.

Fitz-Henley, Samuel A. "The Case of the Missing Court Reporter," *Transcript,* XXXI (1970): 19.

Goldberg, Arthur, and Alan Dershowitz. "Declaring the Death Penalty Unconstitutional," *Harvard Law Review,* LXXXIII (1970): 1773.

House of Representatives, Committee on the Judiciary. Hearings before Subcommittee Number Three, 84th Congress, 1st Session, ser. 6 (1955).

Lewis, Milton. "Hogan's Lie Detector Used 8 Times," *New York Herald Tribune,* April 16, 1961, section 2, page 4.

McGee, Richard. "Capital Punishment as Seen by a Correctional Administrator," *Federal Probation,* XXVIII (1964): 11.

Note. "Remedies for Judicial Misconduct and Disability: Removal and Discipline of Judges," *New York University Law Review,* XLI (1966): 149.

Note. "A Study of the California Penalty Jury in First Degree Murder Cases," *Stanford Law Review* XXI (1969): 1297.

Oregon State Bar Association, Committee on Court Reporters. "Special Report on the Evaluation and Use of Electronic Recording Equipment in the Courtroom," 1966.

Patrick, Claude H. "The Status of Capital Punishment," *Journal of Criminal Law and Political Science,* LVI (1965): 397.

Reynolds, Robert H. "Alaska's Ten Years of Electronic Reporting," *American Bar Associaition Journal,* LVI (1970): 1080.

Sellin, Theodore. "La Peine de Mort aux Etats-Unis," *Revue de Droit Penal Criminel,* VII (1969): 706.

United States Department of Justice, Bureau of Prisons, "Capital Punishment 1930-1970," *National Prisoner Statistics,* XLVI.

Yager, Thomas C. "Executive Clemency," *Journal of the California Bar Association,* XXXIII (1958): 221.

Younger, Evelle J. "Capital Punishment: A Sharp Medicine Reconsidered," *American Bar Association Journal,* XLII (1956): 113.

Book Reviews

Fricke, Charles W. Review of *The Mind of the Juror* by Albert S. Osborn, *Southern California Law Review,* XI (1938): 540.

————. Review of *Elements of Police Science* by Rollin M. Perkins, *Southern California Law Review,* XV (1942): 543.

Index